HOW TO
LIVE AND
WORK IN
THE UK

Visit our How To website at www.howto.co.uk

At **www.howto.co.uk** you can engage in conversation with our authors – all of whom have 'been there and done that' in their specialist fields. You can get access to special offers and additional content but most importantly you will be able to engage with, and become a part of, a wide and growing community of people just like yourself.

At **www.howto.co.uk** you'll be able to talk and share tips with people who have similar interests and are facing similar challenges in their lives. People who, just like you, have the desire to change their lives for the better – be it through moving to a new country, starting a new business, growing their own vegetables, or writing a novel.

At **www.howto.co.uk** you'll find the support and encouragement you need to help make your aspirations a reality.

You can go direct to **www.how-to-live-and-work-in-the-uk.co.uk** which is part of the main How To site.

How To Books strives to present authentic, inspiring, practical information in their books. Now, when you buy a title from **How To Books,** you get even more than just words on a page.

HOW TO
LIVE AND
WORK IN
THE UK

- Guide to UK immigration
- Life in the UK test
- The Points Based System

Mathew Collins &
Nicky Barclay

howto books

Plus
LIFE IN THE UK TEST
Study Guide

Published by How To Books Ltd,
Spring Hill House, Spring Hill Road,
Begbroke, Oxford OX5 1RX
Tel: (01865) 375794. Fax: (01865) 379162.
info@howtobooks.co.uk
www.howtobooks.co.uk

How To Books greatly reduce the carbon footprint of their books by sourcing their typesetting and printing in the UK.

British Library Cataloguing in Publication Data
A catalogue record for this book is available from the British Library

ISBN 978 1 84528 372 8

Cover design by Baseline Arts, Oxford
Produced for How To Books by Deer Park Productions, Tavistock, Devon
Typeset by PDQ Typesetting, Newcastle-under-Lyme, Staffs.
Printed and bound by Bell & Bain Ltd, Glasgow

Copyright statements

Mixed Sources
Product group from well-managed
forests and other controlled sources
www.fsc.org Cert no. TT-COC-002769
© 1996 Forest Stewardship Council

FSC

Contents

Photograph acknowledgements

© Lars Johansson – Fotolia.com   xvi
© David Iliff – Fotolia.com   28
© Nuno Oliveira – Fotolia.com   38
© Dariusz Urbanczyk – Fotolia.com   42
© Rob Ford – Fotolia.com   52
© Michael – Fotolia.com   56
© jeff gynane – Fotolia.com   60
© Mike Shannon – Fotolia.com   74
© Stephen Finn – Fotolia.com   110
© Paul Hebditch – Fotolia.com   146
© david hughes – Fotolia.com   152
© Michelle Robek – Fotolia.com   160
© Sammy – Fotolia.com   198
© Vivalapenier – Fotolia.com   234
© Donaldodacco – Fotolia.com   242
© Lulu Durand – Fotolia.com   266

Preface

If you are a Human Resources (HR) professional responsible for foreign national employees, a student or prospective student, an expat in the United Kingdom (UK) on one of the Tier 1, 2, 3, 4 or 5 categories, an EEA (European Economic Area) citizen or their family member wanting to exercise your treaty rights, a would-be immigrant to the UK or an immigrant/expat in the UK needing to apply for Indefinite Leave to Remain and needing to sit the 'Life in the UK Test' – this book is for you.

The UK Government has introduced substantial changes in immigration legislation, policy, procedures and rules which have affected people applying for Leave to Remain and Indefinite Leave to Remain (or settlement) in the UK. This has included the introduction of a new points-based system and a new licensing system for employers employing foreign nationals and education providers sponsoring international students coming to study in the UK.

This book aims to provide the essential information about the history of UK immigration and how it has evolved to where it is today, information necessary for the 'Life in the UK Test' and guidance on how to prepare to pass the test. The book also includes a comprehensive overview of the immigration rules and policy, information to identify what category would be relevant for various circumstances, and how to go about making a visa application. Information is included for employers on how to comply with the new regulations and information relevant to the foreign nationals they employ. We also include practical information on living in the UK.

The United Kingdom Border Agency (UKBA) is responsible for securing the UK's borders and controlling migration into the UK. The UKBA is an agency of the Home Office. It manages border control for the UK, enforcing immigration and customs regulations. It also considers applications for permission to enter or stay in the UK, citizenship and asylum.

If you are an overseas national wanting to spend time in the UK you will have some form of contact with the UKBA. This may be before departure to the UK by way of an Entry Clearance application, on arrival in the UK at a port of entry, for an application to extend your existing visa, or for an application for Indefinite Leave to Remain once you have entered the country. For the unfortunate, contact may be during departure – forced or voluntary.

For HR departments and professionals this book is an ideal tool to help them to discharge their duty of care to look after and provide practical information for foreign nationals arriving in the UK and to assist them in their induction. For multinational and global corporations managing intra-company transfers and global people mobility issues is becoming ever-more challenging. Even during recession the battle for talent and the competition for particular skills are still creating skills shortages in certain industries.

When someone relocates from one country to another they will experience some form of culture shock. They are in a vulnerable position and are dependent on access to information that will help bring a degree of normality and structure to their new day-to-day life. They will have to adapt quickly to a new culture, and organize and implement a host of new practices to keep life ticking along. They will have many questions but won't know where to find the answers.

Nicky Barclay, my colleague and co-author, and I deal with immigration applications and relocating people every day. My firm, AmblerCollins, has been at the forefront of this global industry for the last 20 years and has a vast amount of experience in dealing with these issues. Today more people than ever move for the purposes of family, employment, business and study. In 2009/10 the UK will probably eclipse more then 500,000 foreign and international students. All migrants are usually information hungry and want to know as much as they can about their new destination and how to carry on their lives in a law-abiding fashion once they get here.

With the introduction of new technology and a demand for the best security to protect UK borders, policy and rules are changing more frequently and faster than ever. Every immigrant will have different personal circumstances, and assessing yourself against the current criteria of a particular category and understanding how a Case Officer may interpret the policy, procedures and apply the rules can be confusing and very costly if you get it wrong. Where you are unsure, you should always take advice from an OISC (Office of the Immigration Services Commissioner) registered immigration practitioner.

We have used our knowledge and experience as registered immigration practitioners to put together this comprehensive overview of relevant information. We hope you find the information you are looking for. It will certainly be one of the best starting-points you will find. If you still have questions or want assistance, please contact the AmblerCollins office in London so we can point you in the right direction.

Good reading and good luck!

Mathew Collins and Nicky Barclay

PART ONE

INFORMATION FOR THE 'LIFE IN THE UK' TEST

The information provided in this section is relevant for those who need to complete the 'Life in the UK' test for the purposes of applying to remain in the UK indefinitely or for UK citizenship.

Becoming a British (or UK) citizen or deciding to settle permanently in this country is an important event. If you are applying for naturalization as a British citizen or for Indefinite Leave to Remain, you will need to show that you know about life in the UK. If you live in England, Scotland, Wales or Northern Ireland, you can do this in two ways: by taking the 'Life in the UK' test or by taking combined English for Speakers of Other Languages (ESOL) and citizenship classes.

The information in this section covers the subjects you must have knowledge of to pass the 'Life in the UK' test. These include an overview of the UK, population, ethnic minorities and the four nations of the UK, government, education, religion, employment and everyday needs.

It is important that you pay close attention to this information, as to pass the 'Life in the UK' test you must answer 90% of the questions correctly.

We hope you find this information valuable and wish you luck in your test.

1

United Kingdom Past and Present

UNITED KINGDOM OR BRITAIN?

The full title of this country is the 'United Kingdom of Great Britain and Northern Ireland' (UK). The UK is made up of four nations: England, Scotland, Wales and Northern Ireland. However, a lot of people say 'Great Britain' or 'Britain'. In general, Britain refers to the mainland and Great Britain includes Northern Ireland, the Channel Islands and the Isle of Man.

The people who live in the four nations are all British. However, the different cultures of each nation are still greatly treasured, particularly in sporting competitions.

UK OVERSEAS TERRITORIES AND CROWN DEPENDENCIES

The UK has 14 Overseas Territories around the world. They range from the tiny island of Pitcairn with its 47 inhabitants, set in the middle of the Pacific Ocean, to Bermuda, which has a population of 62,059 and is one of the world's major financial centres.

The Overseas Territories are: Anguilla, British Antarctic Territory, Bermuda, British Indian Ocean Territory, British Virgin Islands, Cayman Islands, Falkland Islands, Gibraltar, Montserrat, St Helena and Dependencies (Ascension Island and Tristan da Cunha), Turk and Caicos Islands, Pitcairn Island, South Georgia and South Sandwich Islands, Sovereign Base Areas on Cyprus.

The Crown Dependencies are not part of the United Kingdom but are internally self-governing dependencies of the Crown. The Crown Dependencies are the Isle of Man, the Bailiwick of Jersey and the Bailiwick of Guernsey.

LIVING IN THE UK

The UK is an exciting, cosmopolitan, prosperous and progressive place to live and work in the 21st century.

With a population in excess of 60 million, the UK is a growing country, offering a wealth of opportunities to people of all ages, backgrounds and cultures from across the world. Consequently, becoming a UK citizen is much prized.

The UK has a diverse and multicultural population. This can be traced back hundreds of years. There have been a number of key influxes of immigrants. In the 16th and 18th centuries French Protestants (also known as Huguenots) came to Britain to escape religious persecution and hardship. In the mid-19th century many Irish families relocated to escape the potato famine. A large number of Jews came to the UK between 1880 and 1910 to escape racist attacks (pogroms) in the Russian Empire. More recently, after the Second World War, which lasted from 1939 to 1945, the UK government actively encouraged migration from countries in Europe to assist with reconstructing Britain. In 1948 this encouragement was extended to the West Indies.

As the economy began to recover in the 1950s it became apparent that there was a shortage of skilled labour in the UK and the government sent agents and set up centres in a number of countries to recruit bus drivers (West Indies) and textile and engineering workers (India and Pakistan), the latter in particular to fill vacancies in the north-east of England.

During the 1960s and 70s the number of migrants fell as the government introduced new laws to restrict immigration. Throughout the 1980s it became apparent that the largest numbers of migrants were coming from Commonwealth countries such as Australia, New Zealand and South Africa, as well as the USA.

Migrants continue to come to the UK for both political and economic reasons. More information regarding current immigration policy can be found in Part Two of this book.

THE UNITED KINGDOM

The longest mainland distance in the UK is 870 miles from John O' Groats in the north to Land's End in the south-west. The majority of people live in towns and cities. The UK is made up of four nations or countries:

England

England is a country of great contrast and diversity both in the places you go to and in the people you meet. All the regions of England are within easy reach of the exciting capital city, London, famed for first class culture, fascinating history and pageantry, its world-class restaurants and theatre.

Scotland

Scotland is everything you imagine – whisky, golf, romance of the clans and a wealth of castles and historic sites. The Highlands area is one of the last wildernesses in Europe.

Wales

Wales captivates visitors with its rich character and landscapes. The Welsh speak their own Celtic language as well as English and have their own culture, poetry and song, which they celebrate in concerts and unique summer festivals known as 'eisteddfodau'.

Northern Ireland

Vibrant cities with shopping, nightlife and festivals, outdoor activities, fabulous food and unspoilt retreats where you can unwind relax and recharge.

Although English is the main language of all the nations of the UK, people in different areas have many different accents and dialects; for instance:

Place	Accent
London	Cockney
Liverpool	Scouse
Tyneside	Geordie
Birmingham	Brummie

Key facts and figures

The mid-2008 population of the constituent countries of the United Kingdom is estimated as follows:

POPULATION (MILLIONS)

United Kingdom (total)	61,383	%
England	51,446	83.8
Wales	2,993	4.9
Scotland	5,169	8.4
Northern Ireland	1,775	2.9

Source: Office for National Statistics, General Register Office for Scotland, Northern Ireland Statistics & Research Agency

POPULATION BY ETHNIC GROUP IN 2001

	Millions	Population %
White (including people of European, Australian, American descent)	54.2	92
Mixed	0.7	1.2
Asian or Asian British		
Indian	1.1	1.8
Pakistani	0.7	1.3
Bangladeshi	0.3	0.5
Other	0.2	0.4
Black or Black British		
Caribbean	0.6	1.0
African	0.5	0.8
Other	0.1	0.2
Chinese	0.2	0.4
Other ethnic groups	0.2	0.4

Source: National Statistics from the 2001 Census

More than 300 languages are spoken in the UK and the 2001 Census shows that 9% of the total population is made up of ethnic minorities. London is home to 45% of the UK's ethnic minority population, with 29% of its population belonging to an ethnic minority. Other areas of England with large ethnic minority populations are the North-West, the South-East, West Midlands, Yorkshire and Humberside. One in five small businesses is owned or managed by members of ethnic minority communities.

POPULATION OF ETHNIC MINORITY GROUPS IN THE COUNTRIES OF THE UK

England	9%	Wales	2%
Scotland	2%	Northern Ireland	Less than 1%

Facts about the population of the UK

- The native-born English outnumber their Scots and Welsh counterparts by nine to one.

- A Census of the population has been taken every 10 years since 1801. The next Census is due in 2011. The information obtained from the Census is available to the public after 100 years.

- The total net worth of the UK, including financial assets, at the end of 2008 was £6,954 billion. This is a decrease of £177 billion on the previous year.

- Currency is pound sterling (£) or GBP (Great British Pound).

- The number of unemployed people was 2.47 million in July 2009.

- The economy is one of the strongest in Europe; inflation, interest rates and unemployment remain low.

- Inflation rate 1.8%.

- Most people work between 31 and 45 hours per week.

- 7.5% of people living in Britain were born abroad.

- 51% of the population is made up of women and they make up 45% of the workforce.

- The UK is one of the quartet of trillion dollar economies of Western Europe.

- The UK has 23 cultural and natural heritage sites listed by UNESCO.

For lots more specific facts and figures, the UK Government's website for the Office for National Statistics, which brings together in one place a wide range of demographic, social, industrial and economic statistics, can be found at http://www.statistics.gov.uk/

THE BRITISH CONSTITUTION

Proponents of the British Constitution, which unlike the constitution of the United States, is not a single document, believe that this 'uncodified' constitution allows for greater flexibility in law-making. Various institutions constantly monitor each other's powers. We will examine these institutions later. Many believe that not having a constitution 'set in stone' allows the UK to adapt more speedily to change, reacting to circumstances and public opinion.

THE MONARCHY

The reigning monarch, Queen Elizabeth II, is the Head of State not only of the UK but also of the many Commonwealth countries that used to form the British Empire.

The UK is not unique in being a constitutional monarchy. A constitutional monarchy allows the reigning king or queen to advise the prime minister of the day and to appoint a democratically elected government in his or her name. The monarch does not rule the country. All policy is determined by the prime minister and his or her cabinet.

Queen Elizabeth II acceded to the throne in 1952 and was crowned in 1953. Her eldest son, Prince Charles, will accede to the throne on her death. On his death his eldest son, Prince William, will follow. The Act of Accession states that only Protestant heirs of Princess Sophia, granddaughter of James I, may accede to the British throne. No Catholic, those who marry a Catholic or those born out of wedlock may remain in the line of accession. Furthermore, the accession is granted first to the eldest son(s) of the reigning monarch. Although Prince Edward, Queen Elizabeth II's third son, is younger than his sister Princess Anne, he is higher in the line of acession.

The Queen has ceremonial obligations such as opening the new session of Parliament, during which she delivers the Queen's Speech. This speech is written by the government and outlines all its policies for the next parliamentary term.

GOVERNMENT

The government consists of 646 parliamentary constituencies. At the next general election, to be held no later than June 2010, this will rise to 650. Each constituency elects its Member of Parliament, or MP, at a general election or by-election. The political party that gains the most seats (or MPs) at a general election forms the government.

The law states that a general election must occur no later than five years after the first session of the new parliament. The government can call a general election prior to the end of the five years if the prime minister chooses. This five-year term can be varied only by an Act of Parliament ratified by the House of Lords. This is the only occasion when the House of Lords must give its consent for an Act to be passed. This occurred during both World Wars. A by-election will be called if an MP resigns or dies.

The UK now accepts legislation made by the European Union and the judgements of the European Court. An Act of Parliament had to be passed so that the UK could accept these rules.

The House of Commons

There are two chambers in parliament, the House of Commons and the House of Lords. The House of Commons consists of democratically-elected members and is therefore the more important of the two.

Members of Parliament (MPs) currently number 646, although this is to rise to 650 at the next general election, which will take place no later than June 2010. MPs' first responsibility is to the people of their constituency. But they are also responsible for law-making. In addition, they exist to monitor, comment on and, if necessary, challenge the government on national and international concerns.

The prime minister

The prime minister is the leader of whichever political party gains the most MPs (or seats) at a general election. They will in turn appoint a number of MPs to form a cabinet. They traditionally live at 10 Downing Street in London and have a country residence called Chequers in Buckinghamshire. They can be removed from office by their own party or by resigning. However, they normally stand down after being defeated at a general election.

The cabinet

A cabinet consists of ministers appointed by the prime minister to head specific departments within the government. The most important departments and their responsibilities are:

The Chancellor of the Exchequer: All financial and economic matters.

The Foreign Secretary: Foreign policy and diplomatic relations with foreign governments.

The Home Secretary: All internal affairs in England and Wales, as well as immigration and citizenship.

Other offices within the cabinet include defence, health, business, justice, schools and leader of the House of Commons.

The opposition

The leader of the opposition is the head of the party that has the second-highest number of seats in parliament. He or she forms a 'shadow cabinet' that mirrors the positions within the actual cabinet. Although often not in a position to out-vote the government of the day on proposed legislation, the opposition's importance cannot be overlooked. It can criticize the government as well as propose bills itself. Prime minister's question time is held weekly and gives all MPs the chance to challenge the government of the day.

The speaker

The speaker is elected by all MPs and is politically neutral. He or she keeps order during debates as well as ensuring that the rules of the House of Commons are adhered to. The Chief Officer of the House of Commons, as the speaker is officially titled, represents the House of Commons to the monarch.

The whips

The whips are MPs appointed by their own political parties to ensure that members of the House of Commons vote. The chief whip is given the title of Parliamentary Secretary to the Treasury. This allows him or her to sit on the cabinet. Whips also liaise with the speaker to schedule the order of business in the House of Commons.

The party system

The three main political parties are the Labour Party, the Conservative Party and the Liberal Democrats. A person may stand as an independent candidate in an election but usually is unlikely to win a seat in parliament without the backing of the three main parties or one of the parties representing Scotland, Wales or Northern Ireland. To be eligible to stand, a person must be over 18 years of age and be a British citizen or a citizen of a Commonwealth country or the Republic of Ireland.

European parliamentary elections

Unlike the 'first past the post' system used in the UK, the European Parliament favours proportional representation. Seats in the European Parliament are allocated on a total of votes won by each political party. The UK currently has 78 Members of the European Parliament (MEPs).

The House of Lords

Probably one of the hardest institutions within the UK to understand, the members of the House of Lords are not elected. Indeed, until 1958 all members of the House of Lords either received their membership through having an hereditary title (for example, duke or earl), where the title passed from father to son only, or from being a senior judge or a bishop of the Church of England.

Since 1958, however, Life Peers can be appointed for their lifetime only. The title cannot be passed on. Usually these peers are appointed as a result of distinguished service in either the private or public sector.

Hereditary peers no longer have an automatic right to attend the House of Lords. They are allocated a limited number of seats within the House.

The House of Lords exists primarily to debate and suggest amendments to new laws. As it is seen to be more independent of the government, it can act with greater freedom from party political pressure. The House of Commons can overrule the House of Lords, but tends not to.

Pressure and lobby groups

These groups represent a wide range of interests. Their major function is to influence governments on legislation and policy. They can represent a specific interest, such as Greenpeace's campaigning on environmental issues, or have a wider agenda, as with a trade union or the CBI (Confederation of British Industry).

The civil service

Civil servants are responsible for executing government decisions. They are not elected but apply for a position to the civil service directly and are promoted from within. The civil service is expected to be neutral regardless of which political party is in government. Civil servants can vote but are not allowed to stand for office while working for the civil service. There are currently approximately 500,000 civil servants.

Devolved administration

In 1997 the government decided to devolve power to Scotland and Wales. It was felt that Parliament was not fully informed of particular matters and concerns in those two countries, such as education and public services. The Scottish Parliament and The Welsh Assembly were established in 1999. However, all taxation, defence, foreign affairs and social security matters remain under the control of the UK Government.

The devolved administations use the proportional representation electoral system. This is particularly important in the Northern Ireland Assembly. Here the mainly Protestant Unionist majority far exceeds the minority Catholic nationalists. The electoral system maintains some form of representation for all.

The current Labour government came to power committed to a decentralization of power through the establishment of a parliament and executive in Scotland, an assembly in Wales, and the longer-term devolution of power to regional level in England. The Belfast Agreement, reached in Northern Ireland in April 1998 and approved in a referendum the following month, also paved the way for constitutional development.

The then prime minister, Tony Blair, announced on 14 October 2002 that the full-time UK government posts of Secretary of State for Scotland and Secretary of State for Wales, following devolution, were no longer required and their roles could be combined with other posts. The Scottish and Welsh offices were relocated within the new Department for Constitutional Affairs (DCA), together with the parliamentary under-secretaries of state for Scotland and Wales.

Following the Machinery of Government Changes in June 2003, responsibility for the overall management of relations between the UK Government and the devolved administrations in Scotland, Wales and Northern Ireland moved from the Office of the Deputy Prime Minister (ODPM) to the DCA. ODPM remains responsible for the English regions.

Scotland and Wales

The highest priority was given to the creation of a parliament in Scotland and a national assembly for Wales because the demand for decentralization in these countries was stronger.

The government published detailed proposals for Scotland and Wales in July 1997 and these were approved by referendums in Scotland and Wales in September of that year. The Scotland Act and the Government of Wales Act both completed their passage through the UK parliament in 1998 and the first elections to the Scottish Parliament and the National Assembly for

Wales took place on 6 May 1999. The devolution arrangements became fully operational on 1 July 1999.

Northern Ireland

The Northern Ireland Assembly was one of the new institutions created following the Belfast Agreement of April 1998. It was an assembly of 108 members with a similar range of legislative and executive powers to the Scottish Parliament.

The executive and the institutions were set up on 2 December 1999, but were suspended when direct rule was re-introduced by the Secretary of State for Northern Ireland on 11 February 2000. The executive and institutions were re-established on 29 May 2000 following negotiations between all the political parties. Devolution was suspended on two further occasions, on 10 August and 21 September 2001, for 24 hours on each occasion.

The Secretary of State for Northern Ireland suspended the Northern Ireland Assembly on 14 October 2002 and Northern Ireland was returned to direct UK parliament rule. The secretary of state, assisted by his team of Northern Ireland Office ministers, therefore assumed responsibility for the direction and control of the Northern Ireland departments.

England

In England, the government does not plan to impose a uniform system because demand for directly-elected regional government varies considerably across the country.

In the first instance, the government has legislated to create Regional Development Agencies (RDAs) to promote economic development similar to Scottish Enterprise and the Welsh Development Agency. This legislation also provides for the establishment of regional chambers made up of members from local authorities as well as regional stakeholders from other sectors to co-ordinate transport, planning, economic development, bids for European funding and land-use planning.

Local government powers

Local authorities work within the powers laid down under various Acts of Parliament at national government level. Their functions are far-reaching. Some are mandatory, which means that the authority must do what is required by law. Others are discretionary, allowing an authority to provide services if it wishes.

Local authorities operating within statutory restrictions

In certain cases, ministers have powers to secure uniformity in standards to safeguard public health or to protect the rights of individual citizens. Where local authorities exceed their statutory powers, they are regarded as acting outside the law and can be challenged in court.

The main link between local authorities and central government in England is the Office of the Deputy Prime Minister (ODPM). However, other departments, such as the Department for Education and Skills, the Department for Work and Pensions, the Department of Health and the Home Office, are also concerned with various local government functions.

In Scotland, Wales and Northern Ireland, local authorities now deal mainly with the devolved parliament and assemblies.

About two million people are employed by local authorities in the UK. These include school teachers, the police, firefighters and other non-manual and manual workers. Education is the largest locally provided service, with 0.9 million full-time equivalent jobs. Councils are individually responsible, within certain legislative requirements, for deciding the structure of their workforces.

Every part of the UK is covered by a local authority fire service. Each of the 59 fire authorities must by law provide a firefighting service and must maintain a brigade to meet all normal requirements. Each fire authority appoints a chief fire officer, or firemaster in Scotland, who has day-to-day control of operations.

Local government elections

Local authorities consist of elected councillors who are voted for in a broadly similar way to elections of MPs, except that proportional representation is used in Scotland and Northern Ireland. Eligibility rules for voters are also similar to those for UK parliamentary elections, save that citizens of other member states of the European Union (EU) may also vote.

To stand for election, candidates must either be registered as an elector or have some other close connection within the electoral area of their candidature, such as it being their principal place of employment. Councillors are paid a basic allowance, but may also be entitled to additional allowances and expenses for attending meetings or for taking on special responsibilities.

Whole council elections are held every four years in all county councils in England, borough councils in London, and about two-thirds of non-metropolitan district councils. In all other district councils, including the metropolitan districts, one-third of the councillors are elected in each of the three years when county council elections are not held. However, a few non-metropolitan district councils will soon hold biennial elections, with half of the councillors elected every two years. Whole council elections are every fourth year in Scotland, Wales and Northern Ireland.

The electoral arrangements of local authorities in England are kept under review by the Boundary Committee for England, established in April 2002 as a statutory committee of the Electoral Commission. Periodic electoral reviews of local authorities are undertaken in Scotland by the Local Government Boundary Commission for Scotland.

The judiciary

Although parliament creates the law, it is up to judges ('the judiciary') to interpret the meaning of the laws. Government can, and often does, criticize judges' interpretation, but cannot interfere. Judges can agree that the government has acted illegally. If this happens, government has to change policy or ask parliament to change the law. The Human Rights Act falls under the authority of the judiciary. If a public body or an Act of Parliament is deemed to be in contravention of the Act, the judiciary may order the body to change its practices or pay compensation and ask parliament to change the legislation.

A judge or, in the case of a less serious crime, a magistrate is responsible for directing juries and legal counsel (barristers, solicitors) on proper court procedure and the subsequent penalty if the defendant is found guilty. On occasion a judge can direct a jury to find a defendant innocent or guilty, although the jury is not obliged to follow this instruction. The judge cannot make the decision.

The police

There are currently 43 police authorities, or constabularies, in the UK. Although, through what is called 'operational independence', the police cannot be directly instructed by the government, they are limited in responsibility by the law and financial restrictions, which are regulated by the government and by police authorities consisting of locally elected councillors and magistrates. For serious complaints against the police a person may address the Independent Police Complaints Commission. In Northern Ireland, complaints are addressed to the Police Ombudsman.

Non-departmental public bodies (quangos)

Quangos, known more formally as quasi non-governmental organizations, quasi-autonomous non-governmental organizations or quasi-autonomous national government organizations, exist to serve the public without political influence. Although a cabinet minister is responsible for appointments, he or she must be seen to do so fairly and without political bias.

The role of the media

The press, television and radio are the most direct ways of obtaining information free from government interference. All proceedings in the House of Commons are broadcast on digital television. *Hansard* is the official report of all proceedings in the House of Commons and the House of Lords, and is published daily.

The press, particularly newspapers, can and do try to influence government policy and hold strong political views. It is therefore sometimes hard to separate fact from opinion unless the reader is aware of the publication's political allegiance.

The law insists that during elections equal voice is given to all, although there are no rules as to how a politician may be questioned.

WHO CAN VOTE?

As of 1969, these are the criteria for being allowed to vote once you are on the electoral register.

- You must be aged 18 or over on polling day.

- You must be a British citizen, a qualifying Commonwealth citizen or a citizen of the Irish Republic (and resident in the United Kingdom).

- You must not be subject to any legal incapacity to vote (such as being in prison).

EU citizens who are resident in the UK can vote in all elections except general elections.

You can register to vote by contacting your local council election registration office. You can find out where that office is by contacting the Local Government Association.
Telephone: 020 7664 3131 Fax: 020 7664 3030
E-mail: info@lga.gov.uk
Address: Local Government Association, Local Government House, Smith Square, London SW1 3HZ.

They will require your postcode and/or full address.

Voter registration forms are also available from www.electoralcommission.org.uk

Electoral registration forms are posted to every household in the UK in either September or October. The form has to be filled in and returned with information on all those residing at the address and eligible to vote on 15 October.

A slightly different system of registration exists in Northern Ireland. The electoral office helpline number is 0800 4320 712. Freephone: 028 9044 6688. Textphone: 0800 3284 502 Fax: 028 9033 0661 E-mail: info@eoni.org.uk Address: Electoral Office Headquarters, St Anne's House, 15 Church Street, Belfast BT1 1ER.

The electoral register is, by law, available to be viewed under supervision by anyone. Registers are held in England and Wales at council offices. Elsewhere they are held at the local registration office. They can also be viewed in other public buildings such as libraries.

Standing for office

With some notable exceptions citizens of the UK, the Irish Republic and qualifying citizens of the Commonwealth who are over 18 can stand for office. Those who may not stand include members of the armed forces (the Army, the Royal Navy and the Royal Air Force), civil servants, those guilty of particular criminal offences, and members of the House of Lords. Members of the House of Lords can hold public office anywhere but the House of Commons.

Local office requires a connection to the locality where the applicant wishes to stand. Working in the area, owning land or property or being on the local electoral register all allow the applicant to stand.

Contacting elected members

The first responsibility of all elected members is to their constituents. You can find out who your local MP, MEP, councillors, etc. are via www.writetothem.com by filling in your postcode. This is a free sevice.

The details for contacting your MP through parliament are:

Switchboard telephone: 020 7219 3000.
House of Commons information office telephone: 020 7219 4272.
Website: www.parliament.uk
Address: House of Commons, London SW1A 0AA.

Your MP should hold regular 'surgeries' where you can meet face to face and raise concerns of either a private or wider nature. Many MEPs, MSPs (Members of the Scottish Parliament) and assembly members also hold these surgeries.

2

The UK in Europe and the Commonwealth

THE COMMONWEALTH

The Commonwealth is a voluntary organization of 53 countries that support each other and work together towards shared goals in democracy and development.

Commonwealth members are as shown on page 22.

The monarch of the UK is the Head of the Commonwealth.

THE EUROPEAN UNION

The European Union (EU), formerly known as the European Economic Community (EEC), was established in 1957. Six Western European countries established this as they believed that co-operation between countries reduced the likelihood of conflict within Europe. The agreement these countries signed was called the Treaty of Rome.

The UK did not join this group initially and became part of the EU only in 1973. In 2004 a further ten countries joined the EU, with another two in 2006. The total membership of the EU currently stands at 27.

Most countries within the EU have adopted the Euro as their currency, although the UK is still currently using the pound sterling. Citizens of EU member states have the right to live and work in any country within the EU as long as they can provide a valid passport or identity card. Some of the newer members still have to apply for work rights, for example Poland.

Antigua and Barbuda		Jamaica		St Vincent and the Grenadines	
Australia		Kenya		Samoa	
The Bahamas		Kiribati		Seychelles	
Bangladesh		Lesotho		Sierra Leone	
Barbados		Malawi		Singapore	
Belize		Malaysia		Solomon Islands	
Botswana		Maldives		South Africa	
Brunei Darussalam		Malta		Sri Lanka	
Cameroon		Mauritius		Swaziland	
Canada		Mozambique		Tonga	
Cyprus		Namibia		Trinidad and Tobago	
Dominica		Nauru**		Tuvalu	
Fiji Islands*		New Zealand		Uganda	
The Gambia		Nigeria		United Kingdom	
Ghana		Pakistan		United Republic of Tanzania	
Grenada		Papua New Guinea		Vanuatu	
Guyana		St Kitts and Nevis		Zambia	
India		St Lucia			

* Following the decisions taken by the Commonwealth Ministerial Action Group on 31 July 2009, the Fiji Islands were suspended from Commonwealth membership on 1 September 2009.

** Nauru is a Member in arrears.

The governing body of the EU is better known as the Council of Ministers and is made up of government ministers from each member country. This body, in conjunction with the European Parliament, is the legislative body of the EU. The Council of Ministers accepts recommendations from the European Commission and the European Parliament and passes laws about how the EU is run.

The European Commission is based in Brussels, Belgium. This is the home of the European civil service, where draft proposals for EU law and policies are developed.

The European Parliament is made up of members elected by each member country and who take the title Member of the European Parliament (MEP). Elections take place every five years. The European Parliament meets in Strasbourg, northern France and in Brussels, and has the power to refuse agreement to laws drafted by the Commission and to make decisions on the appropriation of EU funds.

COUNCIL OF EUROPE

The Council of Europe was established in 1949, with the UK being a founder member. The Council of Europe has no powers to make laws but focuses on human rights, education, democracy, health and environmental conventions and charters. The most important is the European Convention on Human Rights. All members are bound by this convention and those who break it can be expelled from the Council.

THE UNITED NATIONS (UN)

The United Nations (UN) was established after the Second World War. The main aims of the UN are to promote international peace and security and to prevent war. The UN Security Council has 15 members (including the UK) and makes recommendations on action to be taken against threats to peace around the world.

UN agreements

The three most important agreements produced by the UN are the:

- Universal Declaration of Human Rights.

- UN Convention on the Rights of the Child.

- Elimination of All Forms of Discrimination against Women.

3

Religion

The UK is historically a Christian society. However, everyone has the right to practise their own religion. In the 2001 Census approximately 77% of the population said they had a religion. The table below details the different religions practised in the UK.

RELIGIONS

	%
Christian (10% of whom are Roman Catholic)	71.6
Muslim	2.7
Hindu	1.0
Sikh	0.6
Jewish	0.5
Buddhist	0.3
Other	0.3
Total	77.0
No religion	15.5
Not stated	7.3

Source: 2001 Census

THE CHRISTIAN CHURCHES

There is a constitutional link between the Christian Church in England (also known as the Anglican Church in other countries) and the state. The Church of England is a Protestant church that has existed since the reformation in 1530 which was caused by King Henry VIII divorcing his first wife Catherine of Aragon. The monarch is the head of the Church of England and is not allowed to marry anyone who is not a Protestant. The Archbishop of Canterbury is the spiritual leader of the Church of England.

The established church in Scotland is the Presbyterian Church, the head of which is the Chief Moderator. There are no established churches in Northern Ireland or Wales.

Patron saints

Each nation of the UK has a national/patron saint, and each has a feast day.

Nation	Patron saint	Date
England	St George	23 April
Northern Ireland	St Patrick	17 March
Scotland	St Andrew	30 November
Wales	St David	1 March

The main Christian festivals are Easter and Christmas. Easter always falls on the first Sunday following the full moon (the Paschal Full Moon) after 21 March. If the Full Moon falls on a Sunday then Easter is the next Sunday. Christmas Day always falls on 25 December.

FESTIVALS AND TRADITIONS

New Year

New Year's Day is 1 January. Most people celebrate on 31 December, with people in Scotland calling this Hogmanay.

Valentine's Day

Valentine's Day falls on 14 February and is traditionally when you send the one you love a card or gift. These are often sent anonymously to someone you secretly admire.

April Fool's Day

April Fool's Day falls on 1 April and is a day when people play jokes and tricks on each other.

Mother's Day

Mother's Day or Mothering Sunday falls on the Sunday three weeks before Easter and is a day when children buy cards or gifts for their mothers.

Halloween

Halloween falls on 31 October and is an ancient festival. Traditionally youngsters dress up and go 'trick or treating', asking householders to give them treats or they will play a trick on them.

Guy Fawkes Night

Guy Fawkes Night falls on 5 November and marks the night in 1605 when a group of Catholics led by Guy Fawkes tried to kill the king by blowing up the Houses of Parliament. Bonfires and fireworks are the order of the day.

Remembrance Day

Remembrance Day falls on the Sunday closest to 11 November and is a commemoration of those who died fighting in the First and Second World Wars and other conflicts up to the present day. Traditionally a poppy is worn.

4

Women in UK Society

The role of women in the UK has changed greatly over the last 300 years. In the 19th century women had far fewer rights than men, and before 1857 a woman had no ability to divorce her husband. Before 1882, if a women married, her husband automatically became the owner of all her possessions, money and property.

Women were not allowed to vote, and in the late 19th century an increasing number campaigned for the right. These women were known as Suffragettes, the most famous of whom was their leader, Emmeline Pankhurst. Suffragette activities during the First World War were minimal as women joined the war effort. In 1918, when the war ended, women over the age of 30 were given the right to vote and stand for election. By 1928 women won the right to vote at the same age as men, at that time set at 21.

Women still felt that they were discriminated against in the workplace, with some employers refusing to employ young women or dismissing them if they got married. In the 1960s and 1970s laws were passed to prohibit employers from discriminating against women owing to their sex.

Women make up the majority of employees in healthcare, teaching, secretarial and retail work. However, the range of work women are employed in is widening.

The population of the UK is made up of 51% women and 49% men. 45% of the workforce is female. There are more females than males at university in the UK, as girls tend to leave school with better qualifications than boys.

Historically women would stay at home with their children, Now almost 75% of women with school-age children are in paid employment. In most homes women are still the primary care-giver to their children, although more men are now 'house-husbands'.

5

Children and Young People

There are approximately 15 million children and young people (up to 19 years old) in the UK.

The pattern of family units has changed over the last 20 years, primarily as a result of divorce/separation. The majority of children still live with both parents, though one quarter live in lone-parent families and one-tenth live with step families.

HEALTH CONCERNS

As in any other country, UK parents worry that their children may become involved in using drugs or addictive substances.

Tobacco/cigarettes

The number of adult smokers in the UK is decreasing. However, more young people are taking up this habit, with more girls smoking than boys. Prior to 1 October 2007 it was illegal to sell tobacco products to anyone under 16 years of age. It is now illegal to sell these products to anyone under 18 years of age. Since 1 July 2007 there has been a smoking ban in England, bringing it into line with the rest of the UK, meaning that it is illegal to smoke in virtually all enclosed spaces.

Alcohol

The legal age for buying alcohol in the UK is 18. However, statistics show that the majority of young people will have tried alcohol before they reach this age. There is concern about the excessive amount of alcohol consumed, often referred to as 'binge drinking'. If people (of all ages) are found to be drunk in public the police are able to issue an on-the-spot fine of up to £50, although top doctors in the UK have suggested this should be increased to £100.

Drugs

The UK has strict laws regarding the possession of illegal substances such as ecstasy, heroin, cannabis, cocaine and amphetamines. However, current statistics show that around a third of the population have used these at some time, including half of all young adults. It is believed that there is a strong link between drug use and crime and also mental illness.

SOCIAL ISSUES

The legal age for voting in the UK is now 18. Only one in five young people eligible to vote bothered to make it to the polling booth in the last general election. This represents a fall of over two-thirds on estimates of young voters at the previous general election. Political parties' efforts to attract young people to the ballot box were dismissed as 'embarrassing'. The research, commissioned by the Economic and Social Research Council, examined attitudes to politics among young people who could vote for the first time in the 2001 general election. The survey shows that these young people, now in their early twenties, have little sense of connection with political parties and view them with distrust.

A survey of young people conducted in 2003 showed that they felt the following five issues were the most important in Britain:

- Crime

- Drugs

- War/terrorism

- Racism

- Health

6

Education

Education is compulsory in the UK for children between the ages of 5 and 16. Some children in Northern Ireland and Scotland may begin schooling at four, depending on their date of birth. Parents are responsible for ensuring the attendance of their children at school and can be prosecuted if their child plays truant.

In some areas free nursery education is available from the age of 3.

Education is split into two stages, primary and secondary. In England and Wales, primary schooling is for children between the ages of 5 and 11. In Scotland it is between 5 and 12 and in Northern Ireland from 4 to 11. Secondary education continues to 16, at which age the pupil can choose to leave school or continue to higher education until they are 17 or 18.

Primary schools are usually mixed-sex. Classes tend to have one teacher who teaches all subjects. Parents are encouraged to help children with their learning, particularly reading, writing and mathematics.

Secondary schools again are usually mixed-sex, although there are single-sex schools in some areas. In England and Wales parents make applications to their preferred schools and the school will then look at the examination results of the child and decide whether to offer a place. In Scotland a child will go to the secondary school nearest to where they live.

State school education is free. However, parents are responsible for purchasing the relevant uniform, and charges may be made for extracurricular activities.

Some schools (both primary and secondary) are linked to the Catholic Church or the Church of England. These are commonly known as faith schools.

Private education is paid for by parents and each private school (also known as public schools) will have its own tariffs. There are around 2500 private schools in the UK. Approximately 8% of the UK's children are taught in private schools.

NATIONAL CURRICULUM

All UK schools, state and private, are required to teach the National Curriculum.

The National Curriculum, taught to all pupils, is made up of modules, known as Key Stages. It is organized on the basis of four Key Stages, as shown below:

	Key Stage 1	Key Stage 2	Key Stage 3	Key Stage 4	
Age	5–7	7–11	11–14	14–16	
Year groups	1–2	3–6	7–9	10–11	
English	■	■	■	■	National
Mathematics	■	■	■	●	Curriculum
Science	■	■	■	●	core
Design and Technology	■	■	■	●	
Information and Communication Technology	■	■	■	■	National
History	■	■	■		Curriculum
Geography	■	■	■		non-core
Modern Foreign Languages			■	●	foundation
Art and Design	■	■	■		subjects
Music	■	■	■		
Physical Education	■	■	■	●	
Citizenship			►	►	

■ Statutory from August 2000
● Statutory from August 2001
► Statutory from August 2002

Schools don't have to use these titles for subjects, and some subjects can also be taught together under one name, as long as the National Curriculum is covered. If you want to know more about the National Curriculum for England, visit www.nc.uk.net

Teachers assess children against the National Curriculum levels regularly as they learn.

The National Curriculum Key Stage tests

At the end of each Key Stage there are national tests. Children can't 'fail' these tests. They are intended to show if a child is working above or below the target levels for their age, so that the right plans can be made for their future learning. They also allow schools to see whether they are teaching effectively, by looking at their pupils' performance against national results.

Key Stage 1 tests for seven-year-olds have two elements, teacher assessment and written tests in reading, writing (including handwriting), spelling and maths. The tests are spread out over a period of time, and altogether they last for less than three hours.

Key Stage 2 tests for 11-year-olds also comprise teacher assessment and written elements. The written tests cover:

- English – reading, writing (including handwriting) and spelling
- Mathematics (including mental arithmetic)
- Science

These tests are held in mid-May, and altogether they last less than five-and-a-half hours.

At the age of 15 or 16, depending on the age schooling started, pupils take the General Certificate of Secondary Education (GCSE) examination. Some pupils decide to leave school at 16 to find employment. However, significant numbers go on to take vocational qualifications or Higher/Advanced Grades which will then allow, dependent on results, the opportunity to go on to university education.

While still at school many youngsters take part-time employment to earn extra pocket money. Young people under 14 are not permitted to take employment and there are restrictions regarding the type of work and hours of work.

Careers advice is provided to all children at the age of 14 in England. This is provided from the age of 11 in Wales.

Schools must open for 190 days per year. Term dates differ depending on where in the UK you live. For instance, the summer holiday in Scotland usually begins and ends around three weeks before England and Wales. Parents/guardians are expected to make the school aware if a child is going to be absent for any reason, and if a parent wishes to take a child out of school during term time they will have to make a written request to the school. Student reports are provided to parents every year to allow them to monitor their child's progress. Many schools also have parents' evenings to allow the parents and teachers to discuss any issues or concerns.

University

More young people than ever are continuing their education by attending university. University education is available to those over 18 years of age and the common phrase for adults who go to university at a later stage of their life is 'mature student'.

The main expenses students face are for tuition fees, accommodation and living expenses.

Full-time courses

New and continuing students who started their courses in or after September 2006 will be charged a maximum of £3,225 for the 2009/2010 academic year. The exact cost depends on the university or college attended.

If a student is studying full-time, the main sources of financial assistance are:

■ Student loans and grants from the government.

■ Bursaries from the university or college.

Student loans
Eligible students can get help with tuition fees and living costs through student loans. Students can take out two loans per academic year:

- a student loan for tuition fees, to cover the cost of tuition fees in full;
- a student loan for maintenance, to help with accommodation and other living costs (the amount depends on the student's parents' or legal guardians' income).

Repaying student loans
Student loans have to be paid back, but repayments don't begin until the student has left the course and is earning over £15,000. Once earnings reach this repayment threshold, the student will pay back 9% of whatever they earn over £15,000. If a student is due to start paying back a student loan from April 2012, they will have the option of taking a repayment break of one or two years.

Grants to help with living costs: Maintenance Grant and Special Support Grant
Around a third of new students are expected to qualify for the full Maintenance Grant or Special Support Grant, and around a further third for a partial grant.

Bursaries
Bursaries are extra sources of help from universities and colleges. Institutions in England offer at least a minimum bursary payment if a student is getting the full Maintenance Grant or Special Support Grant. Grants and bursaries don't have to be repaid.

Part-time courses
There are no regulations stating how much universities or colleges can charge in tuition fees for most part-time courses.

7

Housing

PURCHASING A PROPERTY

The majority (66%) of people in the UK own their home, with the remainder renting houses, flats or in some cases a room within a house or flat.

When purchasing a property, most people need to apply to a bank or building society for a mortgage. A mortgage is a loan which is usually granted for a period of 25 years. The two most common types of mortgage are interest-only and repayment.

An interest-only mortgage means you repay just the interest on the amount you have borrowed. Although this is less costly per month than a repayment mortgage, you will need to have available funding for the full amount of the mortgage at the end of the 25 years or the property will no longer belong to you.

A repayment mortgage will cost more per month but you will pay not only the interest but also the amount of the loan, meaning that at the end of 25 years the property belongs to you.

Most people buying or selling property are likely to use the services of an estate agent. Estate agents represent the seller of the property and organize marketing of the property and viewings for potential buyers. Estate agents will usually charge between 3% and 5% of the property's value to provide this service.

If a buyer wants to make an offer on a property, this will be done via an estate agent or solicitor. In England properties tend to be marketed with an asking price and the seller may accept less than this amount.

It is essential when buying a property that you enlist the services of a solicitor. A solicitor will carry out the required legal checks on the property, the person you are buying from and the local area. Your mortgage provider will also carry out checks via a surveyor to ensure that there are no problems with the property. In Scotland a survey is carried out on the property prior to an offer being made. This allows the buyer to put forward a realistic offer for the property.

If you purchase a property you must purchase buildings insurance so that in the event of damage to the property you are able to cover costs. You should also obtain household insurance to cover your personal possessions against theft or damage.

RENTING PROPERTY

The majority of people who do not own their properties rent their accommodation from the local authority (council), a housing association or via a private landlord.

Most local authorities are able to provide housing. To apply for local authority (council) housing you are first required to put your name on the council register which is available at the authority's housing department. A points assessment is then made; if you have priority needs such as being homeless, having children or being in poor health, you will be given more points. Although council housing is available to all, there is a shortage of properties and waiting times can be very lengthy. Social housing in Northern Ireland is provided by the Northern Ireland Housing Executive.

Housing associations are not-for-profit organizations that offer property for rent. There are a number of schemes available, including shared ownership, but again there is usually a waiting list for this type of property.

When you rent a private property you will usually sign a tenancy agreement or lease for a stipulated period of time. This agreement will outline the terms of your agreement and should be read carefully as it is a legal document. It is usual for a private landlord to charge a deposit, which must be repaid to you at the end of your agreement or be used to pay for the cost of any damage/

breakages. The deposit is usually equal to one month's rent, which will have been negotiated between you and your landlord and detailed in your agreement.

At the end of the agreement you must either renew or end the tenancy. If you break your agreement before the date stipulated, you will normally be expected to continue to pay the rent for the period agreed. Equally, your landlord is not able to make you leave the property before the date stipulated on your agreement.

It is against the law for a landlord to discriminate against an individual on the grounds of sex, race, nationality, disability or ethnicity.

Homelessness

If you find yourself homeless you should contact your local authority for help. There is a legal duty on the authority to offer help and advice. You are not automatically entitled to be housed. Help can be obtained from the Citizens Advice Bureau.

8

Utilities

WATER

Water is supplied to every home in the UK. There are a number of companies responsible for providing this service. When you move into your new home you will be contacted in writing by the service provider. You will then be given payment options for your water provision, although it is usual to pay for your water use each month. Your provider can supply a water meter to ensure that you pay only for the water you use.

ELECTRICITY AND GAS

Properties in the UK all have an electricity supply of 240 volts. Most properties also have gas. When you move into a new property you must note the electricity and gas meter readings to ensure you are not charged for the previous occupants' usage. As with water, there are a number of suppliers of electricity and gas and you should obtain independent advice before signing a contract with any new supplier.

TELEPHONE

Many homes within the UK have a telephone line installed. British Telecom is the largest supplier of these services, although there are other companies. There are always offers available and most companies offer line installation and services, mobile telephones and internet services.

If you need the emergency services – police, ambulance or fire brigade – call 999 or 112.

BILLS

You will usually find that options on how to pay bills are provided with the actual bill. Many companies offer discounts to those who pay via direct debit or standing order. Most companies also offer a scheme where they will estimate usage over the year and allow you to make a fixed monthly payment. Services can be cut off if you do not pay bills on time, and a charge will be applied to your next bill if you have to be reconnected.

REFUSE

Each local authority has different days for refuse collection, and most now offer a recycling service. Refuse is placed outside your property either in plastic bags, which usually differ in colour depending on the type of waste in them, or in coloured bins.

For larger items of refuse, such as beds, cookers or refrigerators, you should contact your local authority to arrange collection. A charge may be made for this service.

COUNCIL TAX

What is council tax?
Council tax is a local tax collected by local authorities. It is a tax on domestic property. Some property is exempt from council tax. Some people do not have to pay council tax and some people get a discount.

Valuation bands
All homes are given a council tax valuation band by the Valuation Office Agency (VOA). The band is based on the value of your home. A different amount of council tax is charged on each band. Each local authority keeps a list of all the domestic property in its area, together with each property's valuation band. This is called the valuation list.

Who has to pay council tax
Usually one person in each property, called the liable person, is liable to pay council tax. Nobody under the age of 18 can be a liable person. Couples living together will both be liable, even if there is only one name on the

council tax bill. This applies regardless of whether the couple are married, cohabiting or in a civil partnership.

How much is the council tax?

Each year, every local authority will set a rate of council tax for each valuation band. Not everyone will have to pay the full amount of council tax. There are three ways in which your council tax bill may be reduced. These are:

- the reduction scheme for disabled people;
- discounts;
- council tax benefit and second adult rebate.

Reduction scheme for disabled people

If there is someone (adult or child) living in a household who is substantially and permanently disabled the council tax bill for the property may be reduced.

Discounts

If only one adult lives in a property, they will get a 25% discount on the council tax bill.

Council tax does not apply in Northern Ireland.

Council Tax benefit and Second Adult rebate

You may get Council Tax benefit if you pay council tax and your income and capital (savings and investments) are below a certain level. You may apply whether you rent or own your home, or live rent-free.

Second Adult rebate

You may get Second Adult rebate if the person you share your home with is:

- not your partner or civil partner;

- aged 18 or over;

- not paying you rent;

■ not paying council tax themselves;

■ on a low income.

NEIGHBOURS

Wherever you live, there will be neighbours. Hopefully they will be reasonable people who you are able to get on with. However, if you experience any problems you should consult your tenancy agreement, which should provide guidance on what to do in the event of any dispute. Make a record of any problems, then speak with the neighbour and hopefully a resolution can be reached. If it can't you should contact your landlord.

9

Personal Finance

MONEY AND CREDIT

Currency in the UK is the Great British pound. There are 100 pence (p) in each pound (£).

The Royal Mint is permitted to issue coins in the following denominations: 1p, 2p, 5p, 10p, 20p, 50p, £1 and £2.

The Bank of England produces English banknotes in the following denominations: £5, £10, £20 and £50.

Northern Ireland and Scotland have their own banknotes which are valid throughout the UK. In Scotland there is also a £100 note.

BANKING

Most adults in the UK have a bank or building society account. There are many banks and many different types of account, so you should be sure of all your requirements before deciding which to choose. Opening an account is a relatively straightforward process as long as you are able to show evidence of your identity and proof of an address in the UK. This could be a lease or tenancy agreement or a bill.

CASH AND DEBIT CARDS

Once a bank account has been opened the holder will be supplied with a debit card. There will be a Personal Identification Number (PIN) allocated to the account by the issuer which is required whenever you use your card. You will be able to withdraw cash from cash machines and make purchases with a debit card as long as there are sufficient funds in your account.

CREDIT AND STORE CARDS

Credit cards can be used to purchase goods in shops, on the internet and by telephone. Store cards are similar but are able to be used only in specific stores. If you do not pay the full balance on a credit or store card each month, you will accrue interest. Although these cards are useful, the interest rates tend to be high and it is easy to find yourself in debt.

CREDIT AND LOANS

Banks, building societies and other organizations offer credit and loans. Before you take out a loan or credit agreement it is essential that you are aware of the terms and conditions, as defaulting on these can be very costly. Advice is available from the Citizens Advice Bureau (CAB).

When applying for credit or a loan, the bank, building society or organization you are borrowing from will complete a credit check. If you are refused credit you have the right to ask why.

CREDIT UNIONS

Credit unions are financial co-operatives owned and controlled by their members. They offer savings accounts and great-value loans, plus they are local, ethical and know what their members want. Many credit unions now offer a range of services, including current accounts, benefits direct, ISAs and Child Trust Funds.

SOCIAL SECURITY

The UK has a social security system which pays welfare benefits to those who have insufficient monies to live on. The sick and disabled, unemployed, older people and those on low incomes may be eligible to apply for benefit. You are entitled to benefits only if you are a UK national or have legal rights of residence in the UK.

FOREIGN EXCHANGE

You can change currency in banks, building societies, post offices, exchange bureaux and some travel agencies. You will usually find that a commission is charged, so you should shop around for the best rate.

10

Health

REGISTERING WITH A DOCTOR

Commonly known as GPs or General Practitioners, doctors assess patients, give advice, prescribe medication and refer patients to other specialists. They may also provide contraception advice, sexual health services, maternity care and vaccinations. All GPs have a contract to provide a 24-hour service. This may include a GP out-of-hours call-out service or out-of-hours drop-in clinics that enable patients to visit without an appointment. During normal daytime hours, most GPs work on an appointment-only basis.

You can register with a GP by visiting your local practice and providing them with your medical card details. If you do not have a medical card you should fill in form GMS1, which should be available at the surgery. Once you have been accepted as a patient, your medical records will be transferred to the new surgery and you will be sent a new medical card. When you register with a new GP, it is a good idea to ask for an information leaflet about the surgery, its services and policies.

There are a number of reasons why you may not be able to register with your chosen GP. For example, the practice may be full or you may live too far away. If this is the case, simply choose another GP in your local area. If you have difficulty registering with a GP, the local Primary Care Trust (PCT) will be able to help. You can get the number from the phone book: look under Health Services in the A–Z listing of local businesses and services. You can also get the number from NHS Direct on 0845 4647.

You can register with a GP on a permanent or temporary basis. If you are ill and staying in an area for three months or less, you can register with a GP as a temporary patient. If you stay for longer than three months, you can permanently register with that GP if they are prepared to take you on.

Finding a GP, dentist, optician or pharmacy

The NHS websites allow you to search for your five nearest GPs, opticians, dentists and pharmacies by inputting your postcode.

DENTISTS

Free dental treatment is available to:

- people claiming income support, Jobseeker's Allowance and pension credit guarantee;

- people under 18, pregnant women and women with children under 12 months old.

OPTICIANS

You would visit an optician to have your eyes tested. Most people, except children, people over 60 and those with certain eye conditions, have to pay for eye tests. Eye tests are free in Scotland.

PRESCRIPTIONS

Prescriptions are issued by GPs and prescription charges apply to everyone except:

- children under the age of 16;

- young people under the age of 19 and in full-time education;

- people over the age of 60;

- people who suffer from a range of specific conditions.

Other people may also be entitled to help with medical charges, such as those who qualify for the NHS Low Income Scheme. The NHS also provides a prescription pre-payment scheme, which enables patients who require repeat prescriptions to purchase prepaid certificates (PPCs).

All the information you require about prescriptions and GP services is available through the various NHS websites.

PREGNANCY

Pregnant women in the UK are entitled to received regular ante-natal care. Support will also be available from your GP and midwife. Generally midwives work in hospitals and health centres. It is usual for women to have their babies in hospital, although some women prefer home births. It is not unusual for the father of the child to be present at the birth.

Once a child has been born, the mother will be offered support by a health visitor. The health visitor will offer advice about caring for the child. The initial visit will take place in the home.

You must register the birth of a child with the Registrar of Births and Deaths in the district of the child's birth no more than six weeks from the date of birth. If the child is born to married parents, either parent can register the birth. If the parents of the child are not married, both will need to be present to have both names detailed on the birth certificate.

11

Leisure

Most households in the UK own at least one television and radio and are likely also to have a DVD player, video recorder or some other ability to view pre-recorded programmes. A television licence is required by anyone who has any of the aforementioned items. If a family living in one house has more than one television they will have to apply for only one licence. However, if rooms are rented out in a property, each occupant who owns one of the aforementioned appliances will need to apply for a separate licence.

- A colour TV licence costs £142.50.

- A black and white TV licence costs £48.00.

In some circumstances, there may be concessions on the cost of a TV licence. For example, if someone is aged over 74, they can apply for a short-term TV licence, which will cover them for the period before they turn 75, at which point they become entitled to a free over-75 TV licence.

If someone is blind or severely sight impaired, they can apply for a 50% concession on the cost of a TV licence. Anyone in residential care may qualify for a TV licence at the cost of £7.50 per year.

FILM, VIDEO, DVD

All films receive a UK classification before they are released. These are:

U   Universal: Suitable for anyone aged four or over.

PG   Parental Guidance: Suitable for general viewing but some scenes may not be suitable for children without guidance from parents.

12   No one under 12 admitted unless with an adult.

15   No one under 15 permitted.

18   No one under 18 permitted.

R18   No one under 18 permitted. Films with this classification will be available only in specially licensed venues.

Video and DVD hire shops are located across the UK. The classification of each film is shown on the cover.

PUBS AND NIGHTCLUBS

Pubs play a large part in British culture and are the most popular places to socialize.

You must be over 18 years old to drink, buy or attempt to buy alcohol. It is an offence for any person under the age of 18 to buy or attempt to buy alcoholic liquor or to consume alcohol on licensed premises. However, there are some exceptions. For instance, you are allowed to drink wine or beer at 16 years old with a meal in a hotel or restaurant.

The new licensing laws have allowed many of Britain's pubs, clubs and bars to apply for longer opening licences, giving them flexible opening hours, with the potential to open 24 hours a day, seven days a week. The 24-hour law came into effect in November 2005.

SPORT

The sports the British are most passionate about and take part in are football, rugby, cricket, golf, tennis, Formula One and athletics. With London hosting the 2012 Olympics, it is hoped that many more people will use sport as a leisure pursuit.

Details of sports clubs can be found in your local leisure club or library.

PLACES OF INTEREST

The British Countryside is some of the most beautiful in the world. The National Trust, a charity, works very hard to preserve important buildings and the countryside.

GAMBLING

It is against the law for anyone under 18 to enter a betting shop or gambling club. The UK operates a national lottery which is drawn every week. You can participate in this if you are over 16.

PETS

Cats and dogs are the most common pets in the UK. There are strict laws in place to ensure the safety of animals and instances of neglect or cruelty can result in prosecution. In public places all dogs must wear a collar that clearly shows the name and address of their owner.

12

Transport

DRIVING

You must be over 17 to drive a car or motorcycle in the UK. If you want to drive a medium-sized lorry you must be 18, and 21 to drive a large lorry.

If you already hold a driving licence from outside the EU, you may be able to use it for up to 12 months before being required to take a UK driving test.

To obtain a driving licence you must pass a test, which comprises both a written theory test and a practical driving test.

As a learner driver, before you've taken your driving test, you must apply for a provisional licence. This will allow you to drive when accompanied by someone over 21 who has held a full licence for at least three years. When driving as a learner you must put L plates on your car so that other drivers are made aware of your inexperience. Drivers up to the age of 70 may use their driving licence. Licences are issued to drivers over 70 for three years at a time, subject to a health check.

Insurance

It is illegal to drive without motor insurance. Heavy fines can be imposed. It is also illegal to drive someone else's car if you are not covered by their motor insurance.

Road tax and MOT

In the UK a tax called road tax is payable to drive your car. A valid tax disc must be visible on the windscreen of your car, otherwise it could be impounded and you will be charged for it to be released.

Any car over three years old is required to have an MOT (Ministry of Transport) test. Approved garages offer this service, and will give you a pass certificate once they have ensured the vehicle is roadworthy. Without an MOT, motor insurance becomes invalid.

Safety

By law all passengers in a vehicle must wear a seatbelt. Special booster seats may be required for children under 12 years of age. Motorcycle drivers and their passengers must wear safety/crash helmets.

Mobile phones

It is an offence to use a mobile phone while driving. Offenders will be fined £30 initially, rising to a maximum of £1,000 if their case goes to court. Those caught breaking the ban will also get three penalty points on their licence for each offence. Under current laws, motorists can be prosecuted for using mobiles only if they fail to keep proper control of their vehicle.

Speed limits

Built-up areas: all vehicles, 30 mph (48 kph).

Single carriageway: 60 mph (96 kph) for cars, 50 mph (81 kph) for cars towing caravans or trailers, buses and coaches.

Dual carriageways/motorways: 70 mph (112 kph) for cars, 60 mph (96 kph) for cars towing caravans or trailers.

Car accidents

If you are involved in an accident you must stop. Give your name, address, car registration number and insurance details to the other drivers involved. If anyone is injured, you must also inform the police using the emergency number 999 or 112. The police will ask you for your contact details and a description of the events leading up to the accident. The type of insurance you have will determine whether your insurance company will pay for any damage if the accident was your fault.

IDENTITY

There may be a number of occasions when you are asked to prove your identity, for instance if you are opening a bank account, applying for a job or renting accommodation. The most common documents used as proof of identity in the UK are:

- Passport

- National Insurance card

- Driving licence (provisional or full)

- A recent utility bill

- Rent book

- Benefits book.

If you are a foreign national you can also provide:

- Correspondence from the Home Office confirming your identity and immigration status in the UK

- Identity Card for Foreign Nationals (ICFN), if you have one of these.

13

Employment

Those seeking employment or a change of career in the UK will find that employers advertise roles in a number of different ways. Some employers advertise in the local or national press, others use the job centre and job centre plus, while many companies use job sites on the internet specific to their line of work. Recruitment companies and head-hunters are often used to fill roles which require specific skills within specialized industries.

Employers will often advertise a role requesting that applicants have a minimum qualification level. If you have obtained a qualification overseas, you can have this compared with UK qualifications by contacting the National Academic Recognition Information Centre (NARIC), www.naric.org.uk

APPLYING FOR A JOB

When applying for a job it is likely that you will be asked either to complete an application form or to forward a Curriculum Vitae (CV) with a covering letter to the employer or recruiter. The covering letter should simply confirm your contact details and the job you are applying for. A CV should contain details of your education and qualifications, details of any previous employment and information regarding your interests and hobbies.

It is beneficial to type these documents as this will usually improve your chances of selection for interview.

If an employer is interested in an applicant they will usually ask for details of referees to be provided. A referee will normally be an employer you have worked for previously, or alternatively a college/university lecturer could act as a referee if you are applying for your first position. Referees who are family members or friends are usually unacceptable.

INTERVIEWS

If an employer is interested in employing you from the information they have seen in your application form/CV, you will be asked to attend an interview. First impressions count, so you should always look smart when attending an interview. Within the interview the employer will ask a number of questions about you, your experience and why you are applying for the vacancy. An employer should also provide full details of the role, including salary, holiday entitlement and working conditions. You will be given an opportunity to ask questions. You must be sure you have full knowledge of the position before you make a decision if you are offered the post.

It is imperative that you are honest at an interview. If you are offered a position and it becomes apparent you have been dishonest, you could lose your job.

CRIMINAL RECORD

Employers recruiting for roles that involve working with children or the vulnerable will usually ask for the applicant's permission to conduct a criminal record check. This is usually supplied by the Criminal Records Bureau (CRB).

TRAINING

You will often find that training will improve your ability to secure employment. Many employers will offer this as part of your job, or you can do courses from home or enrol at a local college. The government is currently running a programme called Train to Gain in conjunction with employers in England, and concentrating its efforts on small and medium-sized businesses.

Volunteering is also a good way of gaining experience. There are many organizations that rely on volunteers. You will be able to find details of volunteering opportunities at your local library.

EQUAL RIGHTS

You should not be discriminated against in a job-selection process because of your sex, race, sexual orientation, religion, disability or because you are a trade union member. UK law also states that there are equal rights for men and women, and that if a man and a women are doing the same job they should be paid the same amount. Employment law in most instances does not differentiate between those working full time or part time.

SEXUAL HARASSMENT

It is widely thought that sexual harassment applies only to women. This is a common misconception as sexual discrimination can happen to men also.

It is very important that if an employee feels he or she is being sexually harassed by a colleague or manager, they inform a friend or colleague and ask the offender to stop immediately. It is useful to keep a record of incidents to back up any claims. If the problem does not cease you should inform your employer, as they have responsibility for the actions of their employees in the work environment. The employer should treat any complaint of this nature seriously and take effective action to deal with it. If you are unhappy with the way your complaint is dealt with, you should contact the Equal Opportunities Commission, the Citizens Advice Bureau (CAB) or, if you are a member of one, your trade union.

Sexual harassment can take the following forms:

Verbal
- Comments about appearance, body or clothes.

- Indecent remarks.

- Questions or comments about your sex life.

- Requests for sexual favours.

- Sexual demands made by someone of the opposite sex or your own sex.

- Promises or threats concerning a person's employment conditions in return for sexual favours.

Non-verbal

■ Looking or staring at a person's body.

■ Display of sexually explicit material such as calendars, pin-ups or magazines.

Physical

■ Physically touching, pinching, hugging, caressing, kissing.

■ Sexual assault.

■ Rape.

CONTRACT OF EMPLOYMENT

An employer is required to provide you with a written contract within two months of you beginning employment. This should include the following information:

■ Time off for maternity leave even if you were pregnant when you started the job.

■ Paternity leave.

■ Emergency leave.

■ Time off for antenatal care

■ Protection from dismissal on some limited grounds including pregnancy, whistle-blowing and trade union activity.

■ Working time rights.

■ The right not to be discriminated against because of your sex, being pregnant, your race, sexual orientation, religion or any disability, or for being a member of a trade union.

■ A right to equal pay with members of the opposite sex doing the same or a comparable job.

■ Your remuneration package.

- Entitlement to work in a place which is safe and does not cause you to injure yourself or become ill.

- The right to time off to study if you are 16 or 17 years old.

- The right not to have deductions made from your pay unless you have agreed to them.

- The right to time off for public or trade union duties.

- The right to claim breach of contract if your employer sacks you without giving you the agreed notice, or breaks some other term in your contract of employment.

- If you are paying National Insurance contributions, the right to claim Statutory Sick Pay after you have been off sick for four days in a row.

- The right to be accompanied by your trade union or a workplace colleague in a disciplinary or grievance procedure.

WAGES AND HOLIDAYS

Your salary should be agreed with your employer. However, you have a statutory right to receive no less than the minimum wage or holiday that you are entitled to.

At the time of writing the National Minimum Wage rates are as follows:

- The hourly rate for those who are over 22 is £5.80.

- The hourly rate for 18 to 21 year olds is £4.83.

- The hourly rate for under 18s who are no longer of compulsory school age is £3.57.

Employers who do not pay these minimum rates of pay are breaking the law and can be prosecuted.

At the time of writing statutory holidays in the UK are 5.6 weeks per year although an employer may wish to offer more. An employer can include public or bank holidays in this entitlement but only if employees are paid for these days.

ABSENCES

If you are going to be absent from work, for instance because you are ill or have to attend the doctor or dentist, you should advise your employer as soon as possible. Employers must provide employees with payslips which detail the gross salary being paid and any deductions for tax and National Insurance.

TAX

As in most countries, the UK requires you to pay tax on your earnings. In the UK there is a staggered taxation system, ensuring that the more you earn the more you pay. The tax year runs from 6 April until 5 April the following year and HM Revenue & Customs (HMRC) is the department responsible for the collection of tax.

The first time you start working in the UK your employer will complete and submit a P46 form to HMRC. Until you receive your tax code from the Revenue you will be taxed at the basic rate of tax, currently 22%. Once you are issued with a code, your tax will be adjusted. If your tax code is not adjusted by the end of the tax year you will have to apply to the Revenue to reclaim any tax you consider you've overpaid. Alternatively, if you haven't paid enough tax you will be liable to pay any additional amount of tax due based on your total earnings for the year.

Income tax is used to pay for government services such as the police, education, roads and the armed forces.

NATIONAL INSURANCE

If you work in the UK you will need to obtain a National Insurance Number, more usually referred to as an NI Number. National Insurance will be deducted from your pay by your employer. It is a form of taxation used by the government to pays for pensions, state benefits (sickness pay, disability allowance, unemployment benefit, etc.) and is used to fund the UK's free National Health Service (NHS). People who are self-employed need to make their own arrangements for payment of National Insurance. If you have not paid sufficient contributions it may affect your ability in future to claim benefits such as maternity pay, jobseeker's allowance or a state pension.

UK nationals are automatically issued with a NI number close to their 16th birthday. If you are a foreign national who wishes to take employment you will need to apply for a NI Number by contacting the Jobcentre Plus NI allocation service helpline on 0845 600 0643. They will make sure you need a number and arrange for you to undertake an evidence of identity interview. When you go for your interview you will generally need to take your passport, birth certificate, a letter from your employer or letters showing you are registered with employment agencies looking for work, and Home Office correspondence confirming your immigration status.

PENSIONS

State pension is paid to entitled people who claim it having reached state pension age, and is based on National Insurance contributions.

The state pension age is currently 65 for men and 60 for women. The state pension age for women will increase gradually from 2010, so that by 2020 it will be 65.

The increase in the state pension age will not affect women born on or before 5 April 1950. Women born between 6 April 1950 and 5 April 1955 (inclusive) will have a state pension age between 60 and 65. Women born on or after 6 April 1955 and before 6 April 1959 will have a state pension age of 65.

The state pension age for both men and women is to increase from 65 to 68 between 2024 and 2046, with each change phased in over two consecutive years in each decade. The first increase, from 65 to 66, will be phased in between April 2024 and April 2026; the second, from 66 to 67, will be phased in between April 2034 and April 2036; and the third, from 67 to 68, between April 2044 and April 2046.

HEALTH AND SAFETY

All employers have a legal responsibility to ensure that the work place is safe, whatever the size of the business. All employers must:

- make the workplace safe;

- prevent risks to health;

- ensure that plant and machinery is safe to use, and that safe working practices are set up and followed;

- make sure that all materials are handled, stored and used safely;

- provide adequate first-aid facilities;

- tell you about any potential hazards in the work you do, such as chemicals and other substances used by the company; and give you information, instructions, training and supervision as needed;

- set up emergency plans;

- make sure that ventilation, temperature, lighting, and toilet, washing and rest facilities all meet health, safety and welfare requirements;

- check that the right work equipment is provided and that it is properly used and regularly maintained;

- prevent or control exposure to substances that may damage your health;

- take precautions against the risks caused by flammable or explosive hazards, electrical equipment, noise and radiation;

- avoid potentially dangerous work involving manual handling and, if it can't be avoided, take precautions to reduce the risk of injury;

- provide health supervision as needed;

- provide protective clothing or equipment free of charge if risks can't be removed or adequately controlled by any other means;

- ensure that the right warning signs are provided and looked after;

- report accidents, injuries, diseases and dangerous occurrences to either the Health and Safety Executive (HSE) or the local authority, depending on the type of business.

TRADE UNIONS

Trade unions are organizations that represent people at work. Their purpose is to protect and improve employees' pay and conditions of employment. They also campaign for laws and policies which will benefit working people.

Trade unions exist because an individual worker has very little power to influence decisions that are made about his or her job. By joining together with other workers, a great number of people believe there is more chance of having a voice and influence.

The Trades Union Congress (TUC) has 70 affiliated UK unions representing nearly seven million working people. It campaigns for a fair deal at work and for social justice at home and abroad.

UNFAIR DISMISSAL

If you lose your job, your rights will depend on how long you have worked for your current employer and why you have been made unemployed. Losing your job is a stressful experience and you should take further advice from your union or other advice agency.

There are three ways in which you can lose your job:

- through redundancy (this is when your job is no longer required);

- through being dismissed fairly (this will be because of serious misconduct by you, because you cannot do your job properly or because you do not have legal protection against unfair dismissal);

- through being unfairly dismissed (you can therefore take your employer to an Employment Tribunal). You have three months to make a complaint if you believe you have been dismissed unfairly.

REDUNDANCY

Redundancy is a form of dismissal from your job, caused by your employer needing to reduce the workforce. If you are made redundant you may be entitled to redundancy pay. The amount you will receive will be dependent on the length of your employment. Reasons for redundancy include:

- new technology or a new system has made your job unnecessary;

- the job you were hired for no longer exists;

- the need to cut costs means staff numbers must be reduced;

- the business is closing down or moving.

UNEMPLOYMENT

If you find yourself unemployed you may be eligible for Jobseeker's Allowance. This benefit is currently available to men between the ages of 18 and 65, and women aged 18 to 60 who are capable of and are trying to find employment.

NEW DEAL

Jobcentre Plus offers a number of New Deal programmes to help unemployed people, particularly those who have been unemployed for a long time, people with disabilities or anyone in need of extra help to find work.

New Deal aims to help you get a job if you are out of work. It will give you the chance to train, learn and do work experience so that you:

- can become more confident;

- get new skills;

- can be worth more to people looking for staff;

- can find and stay in work.

More details can be found at http://www.jobcentreplus.gov.uk

SELF-EMPLOYMENT

People who are self-employed are responsible for payment of their own tax and NI contributions. Details of earnings and expenses must be recorded and declared to HMRC each year. Many self-employed people will use an accountant to ensure that their records are kept correctly and that they pay the correct tax and claim all allowances they are entitled to.

MATERNITY/PATERNITY LEAVE

Pregnant women are entitled to time off work for antenatal care. As employees women have the right to 26 weeks of Ordinary Maternity Leave and 26 weeks of Additional Maternity Leave making one year in total. Provided you meet certain notification requirements, you can take this leave no matter:

- how long you have been with your employer;

- how many hours you work;

- how much you are paid.

You continue to be an employee throughout your Ordinary and Additional maternity leave.

Fathers are also entitled to time off when a child is born. To qualify for leave, a father must have been with an employer for at least 26 weeks by either:

- the end of the 15th week before the start of the week when the baby is due, or;

- the end of the week you are notified you are matched with your child.

A father is the:

- biological father of the child;

- mother's husband or partner (including same-sex relationships), or;

- child's adopter or the partner of the adopter.

CHILD LABOUR LAWS

There are laws in the UK restricting the type and amount of work children between the ages of 13 and 16 are permitted to do.

The youngest age a child can work part-time is 13, with the exception of children involved in television, theatre, modelling or similar activities. If a child is offered work in these areas, the child will need a performance licence. Performance licences are issued by local authorities. Before granting a licence the local authority will liaise with the headteacher of the child's school to ensure that the child's education will not suffer should the licence be granted.

Children may not work:

- without an employment permit issued by the education department of the local authority;

- in any industrial setting, e.g. factory, industrial site etc.;

- during school hours;

- before 7.00 a.m. or after 7.00 p.m.;

- for more than one hour before school;

- for more than four hours without taking a break of at least one hour;

- in any occupations prohibited by local by-laws or other legislation, e.g. pubs, betting shops;

- in any work that may be harmful to their health, well-being or education;

- without having a two-week break from any work during the school holidays in each calendar year.

During term-time children may work a maximum of 12 hours per week, but only:

- a maximum of two hours on school days and Sundays;

- a maximum of five hours on Saturdays for 13–14 year-olds, or eight hours for 15–16 year-olds.

During school holidays 13–14 year-olds may work a maximum of 25 hours per week, but only:

- a maximum of five hours on weekdays and Saturdays;

- a maximum of two hours on Sunday.

During school holidays 15–16 year-olds may work a maximum of 35 hours per week, but only:

- a maximum of eight hours on weekdays and Saturdays;

- a maximum of two hours on Sunday.

There is no National Minimum Wage for children under 16.

PART TWO

UK IMMIGRATION

14

United Kingdom Immigration

During 2008/9, the UK overhauled its immigration law and implemented a points-based system for non-European Union migrants wishing to come to the UK to work, study or train.

The new immigration system is split into five tiers that replace the 80 or so routes that have been used previously. Each tier has different conditions, entitlements and entry requirements.

Tiers 1, 2, 4 and 5 were implemented throughout 2008/9. Tier 3 is currently suspended.

Included in the following chapters are the current outlines of the new points-based tiered immigration system. Information is subject to change, so please contact Ambler Collins before making any type of application to ensure you meet the relevant criteria.

The five tiers are outlined below:

Tier 1: For highly-skilled migrants, entrepreneurs, investors and graduate students.

Tier 2: For skilled workers who have a job offer.

Tier 3: For limited numbers of lower-skilled workers to fill temporary shortages in the labour market.

Tier 4: Students.

Tier 5: For youth mobility and temporary workers, such as those who come under Working Holiday agreements with other countries.

Tiers 3 and 5 are temporary migration schemes, and migrants who fall within these tiers will not be able to switch to a different tier from within the UK. Tier 3 is currently suspended in favour of migrants from the EU; however, this may change depending on labour market demands.

Those successful in obtaining Tiers 1, 2 or 4 will be eligible to switch to another tier once they are in the UK if they can meet the requirements of that tier. Tiers 1 and 2 can potentially lead to settlement if the relevant requirements are met at the time of application.

TIER 1 – GENERAL

Skilled migration plays an important part in the UK's effort to keep its economy globally competitive. As part of the UK's points-based immigration system, Tier 1 (General) allows highly-skilled individuals who score the requisite points to migrate to the UK without any kind of sponsorship from an employer.

If you can speak English, have gained a qualification which is at least the equivalent of a master's degree, and can show that you have earned a good income in your home country, the Tier 1 (General) is the right scheme for you.

SPECIFIC CRITERIA

Attributes

The following tables show how points can be scored for specific criteria. A score of 75 for attributes must be reached for an application to be successful:

QUALIFICATIONS

Master's	PhD
35 points	50 points

You are required to provide the following as evidence of your qualification:

The original certificate of award. This must be on the institution's official paper, clearly showing:

- your name;

- the title of the award;

- the date of the award;

- the name of the awarding institution.

Original provisional certificates are not acceptable. The original certificate of award must always be provided unless you are awaiting graduation or you no longer have the certificate and the institution that issued the certificate is unable to issue a replacement.

If you are unable to provide your original certificate

If you are awaiting graduation, or you no longer have the certificate and the institution that issued it is unable to issue a replacement, you must provide the original academic reference and original transcript.

The original academic reference from the institution awarding the degree must be on official headed paper of the institution and clearly show:

- your name;

- the title of award;

- the date of award, confirming that it will be awarded;

- the date that the certificate will be issued or confirmation that the institution is unable to issue the certifcate or award.

The original academic reference cannot be considered as suitable evidence if the letter does not state what qualification has been awarded.

The academic transcript must be on the institution's official paper clearly showing:

- your name;

- the name of the academic institution;

- the course title;

- confirmation of the award.

Previous earnings

Points for earnings are calculated by converting non-sterling currency to sterling (GBP). The sterling figure is converted to points, taking into account the relative difference in the level of earnings between countries. The difference is converted using an 'uplift ratio' that is applied to the entered amount. Different countries have different uplift ratios depending on factors such as GDP per capita, etc.

In pounds per year	Points scored
£16,000 – £17,999	5
£18,000 – £19,999	10
£20,000 – £22,999	15
£23,000 – £25,999	20
£26,000 – £28,999	25
£29,000 – £31,999	30
£32,000 – £34,999	35
£35,000 – £39,999	40
£40,000+	45

You are required to provide the following as evidence of your earnings:

It is essential that earnings are corroborated by more than one source, so you must send at least two of the following from different sources as proof of your earnings:

- payslips;

- personal bank statements;

- letter from your employer;

- official tax document;

- dividend vouchers;

- letter from your managing agent or accountant;

- invoice explanations or payment summaries;

- company or business accounts.

You must send at least two different types of supporting document for each source of earnings claimed. Each piece of supporting evidence must be from a separate source and support all the other evidence so that together they clearly prove the earnings claimed.

For example, when sending documents for salaried employment, you should not send payslips together with a letter from the employer, because these will be considered to be from the same source.

Age

The younger you are, the more points you can score. You can score a maximum amount of 20 points if you are under 28 years of age.

Under 28	28 or 29	30 or 31
20	10	5

You should supply your passport as evidence of age.

UK experience

These points can be claimed if you can prove previous earnings or qualifications gained in the UK	5 points

You should supply the following as evidence of UK experience

Proof of previous earnings made in the UK

There are no specific documentary requirements for claims for earnings made in the UK because the necessary documentation will have been sent to prove your earnings to score points in the attributes area.

Proof of United Kingdom study experience

The specified document is:

an original letter from the UK institution or UK-based overseas institution at which you studied.

This must be an original letter on the official headed paper of the awarding institution and bearing the official stamp of that institution. It must have been issued by an authorised official of that institution and must confirm:

■ your name;

■ the title of the qualification;

■ the date of award of the qualification;

■ confirmation, in order to obtain this qualification, you undertook a period of full-time study equivalent to at least one full academic year, or three consecutive academic terms;

■ start and end dates of the period of study in the UK.

If you are relying on the same qualification you used to score points for qualifications in the attributes area, you should already have sent the original certificate of award, or an original letter from the institution of study. This document will have confirmed your name and the title of the qualification. In these circumstances the letter needs to include only the remaining three requirements.

In addition to scoring 75 points for attributes, it is mandatory that you score a total of 20 points in the next two sections.

English language ability

To be successful in an application for a Tier 1 visa, you must show that you are proficient in English in one of the following ways:

■ You have passed a test in English equivalent to level C1 of the Council of Europe's Common European Framework for Language Learning (equivalent to a grade C or better at GCSE or an approximate overall band score of 6.5 on an International English Language Testing System (IELTS) exam).

■ You come from a country where English is the majority language. This includes Antigua and Barbuda, Australia, The Bahamas, Barbados, Belize, Canada, Dominica, Grenada, Guyana, Ireland, Jamaica, New Zealand, St Kitts and Nevis, St Lucia, St Vincent and The Grenadines, Trinidad and Tobago, the USA.

■ You have completed a degree-level qualification taught in English from a list of selected countries, verified by the National Academic Recognition Information Centre (NARIC), as above. Note that Canada is *not* included on this list. If your degree was earned in another country, information provided by UK NARIC can verify if the English-taught degree is acceptable to satisfy the English language requirement.

Proof of one of these criteria will earn you the required 10 points for the English language requirement.

Maintenance

You are required to score 10 points by proving that you can support yourself and any dependants.

Tier 1 Maintenance Funds	
Applying from within the UK	Proof of £800 in a bank account at all times for three months prior to application. For each dependant an additional amount of £533 must be shown.*
Applying from outside the UK	Proof of £2800 in a bank account at all times for three months prior to application. For each dependant an additional amount of £1600 must be shown.**

* For instance, the main applicant plus a dependant spouse and one child would need to show funds of at least £1866.
** For instance, the main applicant plus a dependant spouse and one child would need to show funds of at least £6000.

You will be required to provide evidence of your maintenance funds. This can be supplied in the form of bank statements. These must be *original,* on a letterhead and must clearly show the applicant's name, account number and date of statement – these must cover the three-month period directly before application.

If bank statements are not available, another option is to obtain an official letter from the bank, stating your name, account number, date, financial institution's name and logo, the funds currently in your account, and that the required funds have been in the bank for at least three months and the balance has never gone below the threshold detailed in the table above. It is important that this information is explicitly stated in the letter.

TIER 1 – ENTREPRENEUR

The Entrepreneur category is a merging of the previous Businesspersons and Innovators schemes. The Entrepreneur category is perfect for those wishing to start a business in the UK and who can meet the criteria.

SPECIFIC CRITERIA

A pass mark of 75 points is needed to satisfy the requirements for the specific criteria under the Entrepreneur sub-category.

Applicant has at least £200,000	25 points
Funds are held in a regulated financial institution	25 points
Funds are disposable in the UK	25 points

You are required to supply the following as evidence of funds available:

The total amount of available money must be £200,000 or more. If money is held in several financial institutions, you must supply a letter from each institution. If money is not held in the UK, the OANDA database is used to convert the amount of overseas money into pounds sterling. The Border Agency will use the exchange rate that applies on the date of the application.

Each letter must:

- be an original document and not a copy;

- on the institution's official headed paper;

- have been issued by an authorised official of that institution;

- have been produced within the three months immediately before the date of the application.

Each letter must also confirm each of the following details:

- that the institution is regulated by the appropriate body;

- your name;

- the date of the document;

- the amount of money available from your own money (if applicable) that is held in that institution;

- the amount of money available to you, or the business that you are running, from any third party (if applicable) that is held in that institution;

- the name of each third party and their contact details including a full address including postcode, landline telephone number and any email address;

- that if the money is already in the UK, it has been in the UK for less than 12 months before the date of application;

- that if the money is not in an institution regulated by the Financial Services Authority, the money can be transferred into the UK.

In addition to scoring 75 points for attributes, it is mandatory that you score a total of 20 points in the next two sections.

English language ability

Applicants must show that they are proficient in English by proving one of the following:

- You have passed a test in English equivalent to level C1 of the Council of Europe's Common European Framework for Language Learning (equivalent to a grade C or better at GCSE or an approximate overall band score of 6.5 on an IELTS exam).

- You come from a country where English is the majority language. This includes Antigua and Barbuda, Australia, The Bahamas, Barbados, Belize, Canada, Dominica, Grenada, Guyana, Ireland, Jamaica, New Zealand, St Kitts and Nevis, St Lucia, St Vincent and The Grenadines, Trinidad and Tobago, the USA.

- You have completed a degree-level qualification taught in English from a list of selected countries, verified by NARIC, as above. Note that Canada is *not* included on this list. If your degree was earned in another country, information provided by UK NARIC can verify if the English-taught degree is acceptable to satisfy the English language requirement.

Evidence of meeting one of these criteria will earn the required 10 points for the English language requirement.

Maintenance

You are required to score 10 points by proving that you can support yourself and any dependants.

Tier 1 Maintenance Funds	
Applying from within the UK	Proof of £800 in a bank account at all times for three months prior to application. For each dependant an additional amount of £533 must be shown.
Applying from outside the UK	Proof of £2800 in a bank account at all times for three months prior to application. For each dependant an additional amount of £1600 must be shown.

TIER 1 – INVESTOR

Under the five-tier points-based immigration system, people can migrate to the UK through the Tier 1 (Investor) category.

SPECIFIC CRITERIA

A pass mark of 75 points is needed to satisfy the requirements for the specific criteria under the Investor category.

Applicants have at least £1,000,000 of their own money in a regulated financial institution in the UK, **or**	75 points
A) own personal assets which exceed £2,000,000 in value, provided they are not subject to any liabilities; and	75 points
B) have money under their control held in a regulated financial institution and disposable in the UK of at least £1,000,000, which may include money loaned to them provided it was loaned by a financial institution regulated by the Financial Services Authority.	

ENGLISH LANGUAGE ABILITY

Because potential migrants applying under the Investor sub-category are not expected to need to work, the English language requirement is waived.

Maintenance

By definition, potential migrants applying under the Investor category are extremely wealthy and do not need to prove an ability to support themselves and their dependants. Therefore, this requirement has been waived for the Investor sub-category.

TIER 1 – POST-STUDY WORK VISA

The Tier 1 Post-Study Work Visa is a route for non-EEA students of higher education institutions in the UK to remain in the UK for two years, upon successful completion of their qualification, to gain work experience.

If the graduate wishes to remain in the UK on completion of two years on this scheme, they must switch to another immigration category such as the Tier 1 (General) scheme.

Students in the UK who have successfully completed and obtained a degree, master's degree, PhD or postgraduate certificate or diploma qualify to apply.

The points-scoring threshold for this type of visa is 95 in total. Of these, 75 points must be scored for attributes with a further 20 mandatory points for English language ability and maintenance funds.

SPECIFIC CRITERIA

Attributes

Has successfully obtained either: 20 points

- a UK-recognized bachelor's degree; **or**
- a UK-recognized postgraduate degree; **or**
- a UK postgraduate certificate or diploma; **or**
- an HND from a Scottish institution.

At a UK institution that is **either:**   20 points

- a recognised or listed UK body; **or**
- on the Tier 4 sponsors register; **or**
- if claiming points for a Higher National Diploma from a Scottish institution, that diploma was earned at a publicly funded institution of higher education or a bona fide Scottish private education institution which maintains records of enrolment and attendance.

Obtained the qualification while in the UK with: 20 points

- Student (Tier 4) leave; **or**
- As a dependant of someone with valid leave in an immigration category permitting dependants in the UK.

Made the application within 12 months of obtaining the qualification.   15 points

You are required to provide the following as evidence of your qualification:

The original certificate of award. This must be on the institution's official paper, clearly showing:

- your name;

- the title of the award;

- the name of the awarding institution.

Original provisional certificates are not acceptable. The original certificate of award must always be provided unless you are awaiting graduation or you no longer have the certificate and the institution that issued the certificate is unable to issue a replacement.

Letter from the awarding body

This letter must be an original letter on the official letterheaded paper of the UK institution where you studied, and include the official stamp of that institution. It must have been issued by an authorised official of that institution and must confirm:

- your name;

- the title of the qualification;

- the start and end dates of your period(s) of study and/or research for this qualification at the UK institution;

- the date of award (no more than 12 months before the date of your application).

If the qualification is an HND from a Scottish institution, the letter must also include confirmation that the qualification is at HND level and was studied at a Scottish institution.

Additional information

If you are unable to provide a certificate of award (for example, when the application is made before your graduation), this letter must also include:

- details of the body awarding the qualification;

- confirmation that the certificate of the award will be issued.

In addition to scoring 75 points for attributes, it is mandatory that you score a total of 20 points in the next two sections.

English language ability

The English language requirement is waived for Post-Study Work applicants because it is assumed English language proficiency was required to obtain the eligible qualification.

Maintenance

Post-Study Work applicants are required to score ten points by proving they can support themselves and any dependants.

Tier 1 Maintenance Funds	
Applying from within the UK	Proof of £800 in a bank account at all times for three months prior to application. For each dependant an additional amount of £533 must be shown.
Applying from outside the UK	Proof of £2800 in a bank account at all times for three months prior to application. For each dependant an additional amount of £1600 must be shown.

TIER 2 – GENERAL

Tier 2 General is for people coming to the UK with a job offer to fill a gap that cannot be filled by a settled worker.

EMPLOYER REQUIREMENTS

If an organization wishes to offer employment to a person from outside the UK/EEA, under the terms of Tier 2 the employer must first have applied to register with the UK Border Agency and have obtained a sponsorship licence.

A sponsor is a UK-based organization that wishes to employ an overseas national in the UK because it has been unable to find a UK/EEA national to fill the vacancy.

If all required steps have been taken to attempt to recruit from the resident labour and there have been no suitable applicants, the employer will need to identify a foreign national with the required skill set and assign a Certificate of Sponsorship to allow him/her to apply for leave to enter or remain in the UK under Tier 2. The Certificate of Sponsorship is not an actual certificate or paper document but a virtual certificate in the form of a database record. Each Certificate of Sponsorship has a unique reference number and contains information about the job for which it has been issued and the applicant's personal details. The Certificate of Sponsorship also acts as an assurance that the applicant is able to undertake a particular job and intends to do so. It is the sponsor's responsibility to provide the applicant with:

- the Certificate of Sponsorship reference number;

- information associated with that reference number.

Live Certificate of Sponsorship

A Certificate of Sponsorship becomes live when a reference number has been allocated to it by the Sponsorship Management System of the UK Border Agency.

The certificate remains live until such time as the applicant uses its reference number to make an application for leave to enter or remain in the UK under Tier 2. If the application is refused, the certificate becomes void.

The maximum period for which the certificate can remain live is three months. This means that any entry clearance or leave to remain application must be lodged within three months of the certificate becoming live.

Only one live Certificate of Sponsorship can be allocated to an individual at any one time.

There's more information regarding applying for a licence and compliance under Tier 2 in the Employers Section on page 129.

Applicant requirements

In order to gain entry into the UK under the terms Tier 2 General, an applicant must:

- have an offer of employment from a licensed sponsor and a valid Certificate of Sponsorship from that employer;

- satisfy the maintenance requirement for him or herself and each dependant;

- satisfy the English language requirement;

- gain 70 points or more in the required points test which reflects the above and other factors, such as academic qualifications and prospective earnings.

The points test

To meet the requirements for entry to the UK as a skilled worker under the terms of the Tier 2 General category, it is necessary to score a minimum total of 70 points as detailed below:

- you must meet the maintenance requirements, for which you are awarded 10 points;

- you **must also** meet the English language requirement, for which you are awarded 10 points;

- the remaining points are awarded for various Attributes (sponsorship, academic qualifications and prospective earnings). You need to score a minimum of a further 50 points.

Maintenance

To obtain the required entry clearance visa to allow entry to the UK under all categories of Tier 2 it is necessary to fulfil the maintenance requirement .This allows an applicant to demonstrate his or her ability to maintain themselves during the first month of residency in the UK.

To qualify at this stage, a migrant must fulfil **one** of the following **two** conditions:

- he or she must be able to show that they have had access to personal monies equivalent to £800 for three months directly before the application is made; or

- he or she must have written confirmation from their sponsor that the sponsor will maintain and accommodate them until the end of the first month of their work in the UK.

If the applicant intends to bring his or her dependent family members with them to the UK, then there are additional requirements: for **each** dependant, **one** of the following **two** conditions must also be satisfied:

- the dependant or the applicant must be able to show personal savings equivalent to £533 for three months directly before the application is made; or

- the applicant must have written confirmation from his or her sponsor that the sponsor will, if necessary, maintain and accommodate his or her dependants during their first month in the UK.

Evidence of personal monies

The following forms of evidence are allowable:

- personal bank or building society statements; or

- building society pass book; or

- a letter from a bank, building society or other financial institution which is officially regulated in either the UK or the applicant's home country.

In all cases the evidence should be original, should clearly relate to the applicant and should bear the issuing institution's name and logo. Statements generated electronically should bear the stamp of the relevant institution on each page.

English language requirement

To gain entry into the UK under the Tier 2 General category it is necessary to fulfil the English language requirement.

Applicants must be able to speak English at a level that shows familiarity with everyday expressions and basic phrases. An applicant can demonstrate the necessary competence in English in **one** of three ways.

■ You have passed a test in English equivalent to level B1 of the Council of Europe's Common European Framework for Language Learning.

■ You come from a country where English is the majority language. This includes Antigua and Barbuda, Australia, The Bahamas, Barbados, Belize, Canada, Dominica, Grenada, Guyana, Ireland, Jamaica, New Zealand, St Kitts and Nevis, St Lucia, St Vincent and The Grenadines, Trinidad and Tobago, the USA.

■ You have completed a degree-level qualification taught in English from a list of select countries, verified by NARIC, as above. Please note that Canada is *not* included on this list. If your degree was earned in another country, information provided by UK NARIC can verify if the English-taught degree is acceptable to satisfy the English language requirement.

Attributes

Sponsorship

If the job you are being offered is on the Shortage Occupation List you get 50 points, meaning that as long as you meet the maintenance requirement and English language requirement, you have the required points score.

If the job you are being offered is not on the Shortage Occupation List you will score 30 points and need to obtain 20 more from the remaining two categories detailed below.

Academic qualifications

You are able to score up to 15 points for your highest qualification:

■ 15 points: PhD.

■ 10 points: bachelor's or master's degree.

■ 5 points: GCE A level or equivalent.

Prospective earnings

You can score a maximum of 20 points for the earnings specified in your Certificate of Sponsorship (this is based on an annual earning figure):

- 20 points: £24,000+.

- 15 points: £22,000–23,999.

- 10 points: £20,000–21,999.

- 5 points: £17,000–19,999.

TIER 2 – INTRA-COMPANY TRANSFER

The Tier 2 Intra-Company Transfer category allows multinational employers to transfer overseas employees to fill a specific position which they have been unable to fill from the local resident workforce.

For this type of work permit, candidates must have been employed by the overseas branch of the company for a minimum of 12 months prior to the application and must demonstrate that the candidate has the relevant knowledge and experience to fulfil the role.

APPLICANT REQUIREMENTS

In order to gain entry into the UK under the Tier 2 Intra-Company Transfer category, an applicant must:

- have an offer of employment from a licensed sponsor and a valid Certificate of Sponsorship from that employer;

- satisfy the maintenance requirement for his or herself and each dependant;

- gain 60 points or more in the required points test which reflects the above and other factors, such as academic qualifications and prospective earnings.

The Points Test

To meet the requirements for entry to the UK as a skilled worker under the terms of the Tier 2 Intra-Company Transfer category it is necessary to score a minimum of 60 points as detailed below:

- you must meet the maintenance requirements, for which you are awarded 10 points;

- the remaining points are awarded for various Attributes (sponsorship, academic qualifications and prospective earnings). You must score a minimum of a further 50 points.

Maintenance

To obtain the required entry clearance visa to allow entry to the UK under all categories of Tier 2, it is necessary to fulfil the maintenance requirement. This allows an applicant to demonstrate his or her ability to maintain themselves during the first month of residency in the UK.

To qualify at this stage, a migrant must fulfil **one** of the following **two** conditions:

- he or she must be able to show that they have had access to personal monies equivalent to £800 for three months directly before the application is made; or

- he or she must have written confirmation from their sponsor that the sponsor will if necessary maintain and accommodate them until the end of the first month of their work in the UK.

If the applicant intends to bring his or her dependent family members with them to the UK, then there are additional requirements: for **each** dependant, **one** of the following **two** conditions must also be satisfied:

- the dependant or the applicant must be able to show personal savings equivalent to £533 for three months directly before the application is made; or

- the applicant must have written confirmation from his or her sponsor that the sponsor will, if necessary, maintain and accommodate his or her dependants during their first month in the UK.

Evidence of personal monies

The following forms of evidence are allowable:

- personal bank or building society statements;

- building society pass book;

- a letter from a bank, building society or other financial institution which is officially regulated in either the UK or the applicant's home country.

In all cases, the evidence should be original, should clearly relate to the applicant and should bear the issuing institution's name and logo. Statements generated electronically should bear the stamp of the relevant institution on each page.

Attributes

Sponsorship

If the job you are being offered is on the Shortage Occupation List, you score 50 points, meaning that as long as you meet the maintenance requirement and English language requirement, you have the required points score.

If the job you are being offered is not on the Shortage Occupation List, you score 30 points and need to obtain 20 more from the remaining two categories detailed below.

Academic qualifications

You are able to score up to 15 points for your highest qualification:

- 15 points: PhD.

- 10 points: bachelor's or master's degree.

- 5 points: GCE A level or equivalent.

Prospective earnings

You can score a maximum of 20 points for the earnings specified in your Certificate of Sponsorship (this is based on an annual earnings figure):

- 20 points: £24,000+.

- 15 points: £22,000–23,999.

- 10 points: £20,000–21,999.

- 5 points: £17,000–19,999.

TIER 3 – TEMPORARY UNSKILLED WORKERS

Under the points-based system, employment-based immigration is broken into five tiers. Tier 3 encompasses unskilled, temporary migration for employment that is largely seasonal in nature.

Tier 3 was designed to replace schemes such as the current Seasonal Agricultural Workers Scheme (SAWS) and the Sectors-Based Scheme (SBS). However, the UK government has stated that Tier 3 will be suspended from implementation for an indefinite period of time.

The UK feels that it can source employees from within the European Union to meet the labour demands of employers who hire unskilled, seasonal labour.

TIER 4 – STUDENTS

The Tier 4 Student category offers overseas students the opportunity to gain recognized qualifications from reputable and government-approved universities and colleges in the UK.

On 22 February 2010 the Border Agency rolled out the Sponsorship Management System for Tier 4. This is an online system which allows licensed education providers to issue a Certificate of Acceptance of Studies, report migrant activity and if required withdraw sponsorship.

To be able to travel to the UK as a student you will have to meet a score of 40 points. These points are scored as follows:

Certificate of Acceptance of Studies from an approved education provider/licensed sponsor	30
Maintenance fees to cover course fees and living expenses	10

What is a Certificate of Acceptance of Studies (CAS)?

A Certificate of Acceptance of Studies is provided by the education provider who is your immigration sponsor. This will include information about you, your sponsor, the course you intend to undertake and your finances.

The Certificate of Acceptance of Studies is not a paper certificate that is supplied to an applicant, it is a virtual certificate which contains a unique reference number that is used on any application forms required to make an application for entry or leave to remain in the UK.

The Certificate of Acceptance of Studies will include the following information:

Route	This should say 'general student' or 'adult student'
You (the student)	• your name (as shown on your passport if applicable) • your nationality • your passport or travel document number (optional)
Approved education provider (also known as 'sponsor')	• the education provider's licence number • the education provider's address • the education provider's contact details • the name and address of any partner institution (if you are studying at another institution as part of this course) • the name and address of any overseas higher education institution (if the time you spend in the UK studying is part of an overseas higher education course)
Course	• the course title • the academic level of the course or the qualification you will receive when you complete the course (the National Qualifications Framework level or the type of qualification – for example, a bachelor's degree). If you will be studying an English language course, the level of the course should be the Common European Framework of Reference for Languages (CEFR) level – for example, CEFR level A2

- the start date (the date you start your main studies, or the date you start an induction or course to prepare you for study if you have an unconditional offer to do your main course)
- the latest date you can join the course (optional)
- the expected end date
- the number of hours per week
- the address of your main place of study, if different from the approved education provider's main address
- the address of any organization offering you a work placement

Evidence used to obtain the offer (Certificate of Acceptance of Studies)

A list of evidence that the approved education provider used to assess your academic ability to finish the course, which may include:

- the level or type of your existing qualification (if applicable)
- the qualification awarding body and/or institution (if applicable)
- confirmation that an Academic Technology Approval Scheme (ATAS) clearance certificate is needed (if applicable)

If you are applying to continue or complete the course of study for which you currently have permission to stay, and your approved education provider has used your progress to date to assess your suitability to continue this course, the education provider must explain this on the Certificate of Acceptance of Studies.

Money (also known as maintenance)

- course fees for the first year, or the length of the course
- course fees that you have paid so far (if applicable)
- accommodation fees that you have paid so far (if applicable)

Will I be allowed to work?

Work entitlement is dictated by the level of course you choose to undertake. Those choosing to study for a Degree Level Course (NQF Level 6 or above) are entitled to take employment for up to 20 hours per week within term time.

You are not allowed to engage in the following:

- work for more than 20 hours per week during term time unless it is for a work placement and is part of the study programme agreed with your education provider;
- conduct business, be self-employed or provide services as a professional sports person or entertainer;
- work full time in a permanent job.

If the course of study you choose to undertake is a course that is below Degree Level (NQF 5 or below) you are only allowed to work for 10 hours per week within term time.

You are not allowed to engage in the following:

- work for more than 10 hours per week during term time unless it is for a work placement and is part of the study programme agreed with your education provider;
- conduct business, be self-employed or provide services as a professional sports person or entertainer;
- work full time in a permanent job.

Regardless of the work restriction during term time all Tier 4 (General) students are allowed to work full time within holiday periods.

Length of visa

The Tier 4 Student Visa will not allow you to apply to settle in the UK, however, it may allow you to switch to another category of visa upon successful completion of your studies, for instance Tier 1 Post-Study Work.

How long will my visa be issued for?

Type of course	Length of course	Length of stay allowed
Degree level or above	12 months or more	The full length of the course plus four months after the end of your course
Degree level or above	Six months or more, but less than 12 months	The full length of the course plus two months after the end of your course

Course to prepare you for study (known as pre-sessional)	Less than six months	The full length of the course plus one month after the end of your course
Short course (not one to prepare you for study)	Less than six months	The full length of the course plus seven days after the end of your course
Below degree level	12 months or more	The full length of the course (up to a maximum of three years if you are 18 years old or over) plus four months after the end of your course
Below degree level	Six months or more, but less than 12 months	The full length of the course (up to a maximum of three years if you are 18 years old or over) plus two months after the end of your course
Postgraduate doctors and dentists on a recognised Foundation programme	Maximum of three years	The full length of the course (up to a maximum of three years) plus one month after the end of your course

How much money do I need to study in the UK if I am applying from outside the UK for entry clearance?

Length of course	Where you will study	Maintenance (funds) needed
Nine months or less	In London	Course fees **and** £800 to cover living costs for each calendar month of the course
Nine months or less	Outside London	Course fees **and** £600 to cover living costs for each calendar month of the course
More than nine months	In London	First year of fees **and** £7,200 to cover living costs for nine months in the UK
More than nine months	Outside London	First year of fees **and** £5,400 to cover living costs for nine months in the UK

How much money do I need if I want to extend my stay in the UK as a student and I have completed, in the past four months, a course of study in the UK that was at least six months long?

You may need to show a lower amount of money for your living costs if:

■ you have done a course of study in the UK in the last four months before you apply, or you are currently studying and need more time to finish your course;

■ that course was six months or more in length;

■ you want to apply for permission to stay for a further period as an adult student.

If you meet all of these requirements, you only need to show the amount of money below for your living costs, whether you are applying from inside the UK (for an extension) or from overseas.

Length of course	Where you will study	Money needed
Nine months or less	Inner London	Course fees **and** £800 to cover living costs for each calendar month of the course up to a maximum of two months
Nine months or less	Outer London or anywhere else in the UK	Course fees **and** £600 to cover living costs for each calendar month of the course up to a maximum of two months
More than nine months	Inner London	First year of fees **and** £1,600 to cover two months of living costs in the UK
More than nine months	Outer London or anywhere else in the UK	First year of fees **and** £1,200 to cover two months of living costs in the UK

You are required to show that you have had access to the funds detailed above at all times for at least 28 days directly before making your application.

Dependants

Tier 4 (General) students who will be studying for 6 months or less are not allowed to bring their partners/children (dependants) to the UK with them.

Tier 4 (General) students who will be studying a course lower than Degree level (excluding foundation degree courses), but for more than 6 months are allowed to bring their partners/children (dependants) to the UK with them, however dependants are now allowed to take employment unless they are able to qualify in their own right to enter the UK under Tier 1 or 2 of the Points Based System.

Tier 4 (General) students studying a Degree level course for longer than 6 months are allowed to bring their partners/children (dependants) to the UK with them, and the dependants are entitled to take employment.

TIER 5 – TEMPORARY WORKERS

Tier 5 Visas

Tier 5 of the points-based system is designed to allow temporary workers and 18–30 year-olds in the Youth Mobility Scheme to come to the UK to undertake short-term, temporary work to satisfy essentially non-financial objectives.

Tier 5 is designed to ensure the UK will continue to receive the cultural, social, religious and international development benefits of particular types of temporary workers and youth mobility.

Under Tier 5 – applicants may apply through one of the following categories:

Creative and sporting worker category

The creative and sporting worker category is for people coming to the UK to work or perform as sports people, entertainers or creative artists for up to 12 months.

If you are a sports person, you must be internationally established at the highest level in your sport, and/or your job must make a significant contribution to the development and running of sport at the highest level in the UK. If you are a coach, you must be suitably qualified to do the job.

Charity worker category

The charity worker category is for people coming to the UK to undertake voluntary work for charity, which is not paid work. The work must be directly related to the work of your sponsor's organization.

Religious worker category

The religious worker category is for people coming to the UK to work temporarily as a religious worker.

Religious workers can do:

- preaching, pastoral work and non-pastoral work;
- work in the UK in the same way as the applicant is working in an overseas organization (although your duties in the UK may be different); the job should be done during a break from your job overseas;
- work in a religious order which involves a permanent commitment, like a monastery or convent. The work in a religious order must be in the order itself or in outside work directed by the order. You can apply if you are a novice whose training means taking part in the daily community life of the order.

Government-authorised exchange category

The government-authorised exchange category is for people coming to the UK through approved schemes that aim to share knowledge, experience and best practice, and to experience the social and cultural life of the UK. This category must not be used to fill job vacancies or to bring unskilled labour to the UK.

Your sponsor will be an overarching body that manages the government-authorised exchange scheme. This overarching body must have the support of a UK government department.

Individual employers and organizations will not be allowed to sponsor migrants in this category, even if they are licensed as sponsors under other tiers or other categories of Tier 5. The only exceptions to this are if you are coming to the UK:

- as a sponsored researcher, where the higher education institution you are coming to work at will be your sponsor;
- to work for a government department or agency.

Any work you do must be skilled, which means it must be equivalent to NVQ or SVQ level 3 or above. This is unless you are taking part in the scheme set up as part of the EU's lifelong learning programme, where you can do vocational education and training at a lower skill level.

You are allowed to stay in the UK for up to 24 months under this category.

International agreement category

The international agreement category is for people coming to the UK under contract to do work that is covered under international law, including:

- the General Agreement on Trade in Services (GATS);
- similar agreements between the UK and another country;
- employees of overseas governments and international organisations;
- private servants in diplomatic households.

Youth Mobility Scheme

The Youth Mobility Scheme is for young people from participating countries who would like to experience life in the UK. The countries in the scheme are:

- Australia;
- Canada;
- Japan;
- New Zealand.

Under the Youth Mobility Scheme, your national government is your sponsor. British overseas citizens, British overseas territories citizens and British nationals (overseas) can also apply under the scheme and do not need a sponsor.

15

Spouses, Fiancé(e)s and Unmarried Partners

How do I qualify to join my spouse or partner in the UK?

You qualify if you can prove that:

- you are legally married to each other or are in a de facto partnership recognised in the UK;

- your spouse or partner is present and settled in the UK*;

- you intend to live together permanently as spouses or de facto partners;

- you have met each other before;

- together you can support yourselves and any dependants without assistance from public funds;

- you have suitable accommodation, which is owned or lived in only by you and your household, and where you and your dependants can live without any assistance from public funds;

- your spouse or partner is not under 21;

- you are not under 21.

* 'Settled' means being allowed to live in the UK lawfully, with no time limit on your stay. 'Present and settled' means that the person concerned is settled in the UK and, at the time your application is made, is either in the UK or is intending to come here with you, or to join you and plans to live with you in the UK if your application is successful.

If your husband or wife has more than one wife or husband, only one will be allowed to join them in the UK.

Initially, you will be allowed to stay and work in the UK for two years. Towards the end of this period, if you are still married and intend to continue living together, you are able to make an application to the UK Border Agency to stay in the UK permanently.

If you and your spouse or de facto partner have been living together outside the UK for four years or more, and they have been a British citizen for four years or more, there is no limit to the time you can stay in the UK.

How do I qualify to join my fiancé, fiancée or proposed partner in the UK?

You qualify if you can prove that:

- you plan to marry or register a civil partnership within a reasonable time (usually six months);

- you intend to live together permanently after you are married or have registered a civil partnership;

- you have met each other before;

- there is somewhere for you and your dependants to live until you get married or register a civil partnership, and you will be able to live without assistance from public funds;

- you and your dependants can be supported without working or claiming any assistance from public funds.

You will be allowed to stay in the UK for six months but do not have permission to take employment within this period. When you are married or have registered a civil partnership, you can apply for a two-year extension to your visa and, if your application is granted, you will be allowed to take employment without restriction. Towards the end of this period, you are able to make an application to the UK Border Agency to stay in the UK permanently.

How do I qualify to join my unmarried or same-sex partner in the UK?

You qualify if you can prove that:

■ your partner currently lives and is settled in the UK, or that they are going to live permanently in the UK;

■ both you and your partner are over 21 years of age;

and that:

■ any previous marriages or civil partnerships, have permanently broken down;

■ you have been living together in a relationship similar to marriage or civil partnership for two years or more;

■ you have suitable accommodation which is owned or lived in only by you and your household, and where you and your dependants can live without any assistance from public funds;

■ you can support yourselves and any dependants without any help from public funds;

■ you intend to live together permanently;

■ both you and your partner are over 21 years of age.

Initially, you will be allowed to stay and work in the UK for two years. Towards the end of this period, if you are still married and intend to continue living together, you are able to make an application to the UK Border Agency to stay in the UK permanently.

If you and your unmarried or same-sex partner have been living together outside the UK for four years or more, and they have been a British citizen for four years or more, there will be no time limit to how long you can stay in the UK.

16

EEA Nationals

The following countries are members of the European Economic Area (EEA).

Austria	Greece	Netherlands
Belgium	Hungary**	Norway
Bulgaria*	Iceland	Poland**
Cyprus	Ireland	Portugal
Czech Republic**	Italy	Romania*
Denmark	Latvia**	Slovakia**
Estonia*	Liechtenstein	Slovenia**
Finland	Lithuania**	Spain
France	Luxembourg	Sweden
Germany	Malta	United Kingdom

* Nationals from these countries are required to apply for permission to work before starting any job in the UK.
** Nationals from these countries will have to register under the Worker Registration Scheme.

Do I have a right of residence in the UK?

European Community law gives EEA nationals a right to live and work in the UK. This is called a right of residence.

You have the right of residence in the UK if you are an EEA national and:

■ you are working in the UK;

■ you do not work in the UK but you have enough money to support yourself for the whole period of your stay without assistance from public funds.

How do I prove my nationality when entering the UK?

You will need to show your passport or national identity card. When you arrive at UK ports and airports, you should use the separate channel marked 'EEA/EU' where it is available. Immigration Officers will check your passport or national identity card to make sure that it is valid and that it belongs to you.

What rights do I have if I want to work in the UK?

You can:

■ accept offers for work;

■ work (in employment or self-employment);

■ set up in business;

■ manage a company;

■ set up a local branch of a company.

You do not need a work permit, but you may need to register as a worker under the Worker Registration Scheme.

Can I live in the UK if I am not working?

You can live in the UK without working; for example, as a student or a retired person.

You must have enough money to support yourself through the whole period of your stay so that you do not need assistance from public funds.

Can I work in the UK if I am studying?

Yes. You can work in the UK during or after finishing your studies, although you may need to register as a worker under the Worker Registration Scheme.

Do I need to apply for a residence permit or register with the police?

No. If you have the right to live in the UK, you can stay for as long as you want without getting a residence permit or registering with the police.

However, if you choose to do so, you can apply to the Immigration and Nationality Directorate for a residence permit. This simply confirms that you have the right to live in the UK under European Community law.

A residence permit is normally valid for five years. However, it may be issued for shorter periods if you are working or studying in the UK for less than 12 months.

You will not normally be granted a residence permit if you:

- are in the UK for a short visit;

- are looking for work;

- will work and live in the UK for less than three months;

- do not work in the UK and you cannot support yourself without help from public funds;

- have been registered on the Worker Registration Scheme for less than 12 months.

YOUR FAMILY'S RIGHTS

If your family members are EEA nationals they will have the same rights as you to live and work in the UK.

The following information applies to family members who are not EEA nationals.

Can my family join me in the UK?

Yes. If you have the right to live in the UK your family can join you.

Under European Community law, your family includes:

- your spouse;

- your spouse's children or grandchildren (if they are under 21 years of age or if they are over 21 and are dependent on you);

■ dependent relatives, for example your spouse's parents or grandparents.

If you are a student, only your husband or wife and your dependent children can join you.

An unmarried partner is not eligible for an EEA family permit.

Can my other relatives join me in the UK?

Your other relatives, such as brothers, sisters, cousins and so on, do not have an automatic right to live in the UK with you. However, applications will be considered if you are working or coming to work in the UK and:

■ they are dependent on you; or

■ they were living with you before you came to the UK; or

■ they are living with you now outside of the UK.

How can my family come to live with me in the UK?

Non-EEA family members must obtain an EEA family permit before they travel to the UK if they are coming to live with you permanently or on a long-term basis. If they try to enter the UK for this purpose without an EEA family permit, they may be refused entry.

What is an EEA family permit?

An EEA family permit is a form of entry clearance that allows members of your family who are not EEA nationals to travel with you or join you in the UK.

Can my family members take employment in the UK?

Yes. A family member of an EEA national who is exercising their rights under EU law can take employment.

Can my family lose their right to stay in the UK?

Your family could lose their right of residence in the UK if:

■ you no longer have the right of residence in the UK;

- you leave the UK permanently;

- you are not working in the UK and you cannot live in the UK without getting help from public funds.

Your husband or wife may also lose the right to stay in the UK if you are divorced.

Do I have to be present when my family members apply for a family permit?

No. As long as your family member has all of the relevant documents, they can apply without you needing to be present.

ANCESTRY VISA

How do I qualify for UK ancestry?

You qualify if you can prove that:

- you are a Commonwealth citizen;

- you are aged 17 or over;

- you have a grandparent who was born in the UK, the Channel Islands or the Isle of Man;

- you have a grandparent who was born in what is now the Republic of Ireland before 31 March 1922;

- you are able to work and intend to do so in the UK;

- you can support yourself and any dependants, and live without needing any help from public funds.

NB: If you or your parent (who you are claiming ancestry through) is adopted, you are still able to apply for entry under this category. You must show evidence of the legal adoption with your application form.

Do I need to obtain a work permit?

No. You do not need a work permit.

How long can I stay?

If you arrive with a UK Ancestry visa, you have permission to stay for an initial period of five years.

What happens after five years?

After five years, you will be able to apply for permanent residency.

You are able to apply for permanent residency as long as:

- you continue to meet the requirements of the Rules for United Kingdom Ancestry, and

- you have spent a period of five years in employment in the UK in this way, without a lengthy break.

An application for permanent residence is made to the UK Border Agency.

Can my family join me in the UK?

Your husband, wife or eligible partner and children under 18 years of age can join you in the UK if:

- they have a visa for this purpose;

- you can support them and live without any help from public funds.

VISITOR'S VISA

How do I qualify to travel to the UK as a visitor?

You must be able to prove that:

- you want to visit the UK for no more than six months;

- you intend to leave the UK at the end of your visit;

- you have enough money to support yourself and live in the UK without working or assistance from public funds.

You will need to obtain a visa to visit the UK if you:

- are from a visa national country (this information can be found on www.ukvisas.gov.uk);

- are stateless (you do not have a nationality);

- hold a non-national travel document (a travel document which does not give you the nationality of the country that issued it);

- hold a passport issued by an authority that is not recognized in the UK.

What am I allowed to do within my time as a visitor?

As a visitor, you can:

- go to meetings and trade fairs, buy goods, and negotiate and complete contracts with UK businesses;

- go to conferences and seminars as a delegate;

- find out about, check the details of or examine goods;

- get training as long as it is classroom-based instruction or limited to observation only.

In limited circumstances you can also enter the UK as a visitor if you are:

- delivering goods from abroad;

- a representative of a foreign company coming to service, repair or install products;

- an adviser, consultant, trainer or other kind of specialist who is employed abroad either directly or under contract by the same company or group of companies;

- a guest speaker or expert speaker at a conference or seminar or you are running a conference or seminar for no more than five days;

- a sportsperson or entertainer travelling for trials, auditions or personal appearances that do not involve performances.

You cannot:

- take paid or unpaid work;

- produce goods or provide services in the UK;

- sell goods and services to members of the public.

Can I study in the UK?

Yes, as a visitor you can study during your stay.

Can I get married or register a civil partnership in the UK?

If either you or your future spouse or proposed civil partner are **not** EEA citizens you can visit the UK together to get married or register a civil partnership as long as you intend to leave the country within six months.

Can I get medical treatment in the UK?

Yes. You can apply for a visit visa to travel to the UK for private medical treatment as long as you can prove that you:

- have made suitable arrangements for the necessary consultation or treatment;

- have enough money to pay for the treatment;

- have enough money to support yourself and live without working or assistance from public funds while you are in the UK;

- intend to leave the UK at the end of your treatment.

17

Entry Clearance

The visas detailed on the preceding pages require citizens of all Visa National Countries and those of any other country who wish to enter the UK for more than 6 months to make an application for Entry Clearance prior to travelling to the UK.

The following information will give you a better understanding of this process and should answer any questions you may have.

WHAT IS A VISA?

A visa is a certificate that is put into your passport or travel document at a British mission overseas. The visa gives you permission to enter the UK. If you have a valid UK visa you will not normally be refused entry to the UK unless your circumstances have changed, or you have provided false information or you did not disclose important facts when you applied for your visa.

When you arrive in the UK, an immigration officer may ask you questions. It is therefore advisable to have all relevant documentation in your hand luggage.

HOW DO I APPLY FOR A VISA?

You are required to complete a visa application form. These forms can be obtained from any British Mission overseas or can be downloaded at www.ukvisas.gov.uk (there is no charge for these forms). You should apply for a visa in the country of which you are a national or where you legally live.

You can apply in a number of ways: by post, by courier, in person and online. The visa section of the British Mission in the country from which you need to apply will advise which of these options are available.

What do I need to make my application?

You will need to supply the following.

- correctly-completed application form;

- your passport or travel document;

- a recent passport-sized (45mm x 35mm) colour photograph of yourself; this should be:
  - taken against a light coloured background
  - clear and of good quality, and not framed or backed
  - printed on normal photographic paper
  - full face and without sunglasses, hat or other head covering unless you wear this for cultural or religious reasons;

- the visa fee; this cannot be refunded, and you must normally pay it in the local currency of the country where you are applying;

- any relevant supporting documents.

All UK visa applicants, save for those benefiting from a limited number of exemptions and exceptions, are required to provide biometric data (10-digit fingerscans and a digital photograph) as part of the application process.

What supporting documents should I include with my application?

You should include all the documents you can to show that you qualify for entry to the UK in the category in which you are applying.

What happens when I make my application?

The Entry Clearance Officer will try to make a decision using your application form and the supporting documents you have provided. If this is not possible, they will need to interview you.

If your application is successful, you will be issued with a visa. It is imperative that you check your visa to make sure that:

- your personal details are correct;

- it correctly states the purpose for which you want to come to the UK;

■ it is valid for the date on which you want to travel you can ask for it to be post-dated for up to three months if you do not plan to travel immediately.

If you think there is anything wrong with your visa, you must contact the visa section that processed your application immediately.

INDEFINITE LEAVE TO REMAIN

Full or permanent residency is properly known as Indefinite Leave to Remain (ILR). You can apply for this in several ways, depending on your UK immigration status at the time of application.

Indefinite Leave to Remain allows the holder to remain in the UK for an indefinite period, on the condition that he/she intends to remain present and settled. If you have been granted Indefinite Leave to Remain and leave the UK for a period of two years or more, it is usually deemed that you are not present and settled and therefore your ILR status will be revoked.

Indefinite Leave to Remain allows the holder to work without restriction in the UK. It also allows exit and re-entry on multiple occasions.

The following are some ways in which an individual may apply for Indefinite Leave to Remain:

■ shortly before the expiry of a two-year marriage visa;

■ on the basis of being married to or in a relationship for four years or more with a British citizen or a person who has no time limitation on their ability to stay in the UK;

■ shortly before the expiry of a five-year Ancestry Visa;

■ once having held a Tier 1/Tier 2 visa for a five-year period;

■ once having legally spent ten years in the UK;

■ once having spent 14 years in the UK;

■ once having spent five continuous years as a representative of an overseas newspaper, news agency or broadcasting organization.

- once having spent five years in the UK as a sole representative;

- once having spent five years in the UK as an overseas government employee or servant in a diplomatic household;

- once having spent five years in the UK as a minister of religion, missionary or member of a religious order;

- once having spent a continuous five-year period in the UK as a member of the operational ground staff of an overseas-owned airline;

- once having spent a continuous five-year period in the UK as a person established in business under the provisions of the EU Association Agreement;

- once having spent a continuous five years in the UK as an investor or retired person of independent means;

- once having spent a continuous five years in the UK as a writer, composer or artist;

- an EEA national and the family members of this person may apply for ILR if they have been issued with a residence permit or document for five years; they must have remained, and intend to continue to do so, in the UK for at least five years.

In most circumstances you must have passed the 'Life in the UK' test to be in a position to apply for Indefinite Leave to Remain. You will find information regarding the 'Life in the UK' test in Part 1 of this book.

LONG RESIDENCY VISA

The Long Residency Visa is divided into two types: the 10 Year Visa and the 14 Year Visa.

The 10 Year Visa may be considered if the applicant has been legally resident in the UK with Home Office approval for ten years. Usually, if successful, the applicant will be allowed to remain in the UK without time limitation, and granted Indefinite Leave To Remain (ILR).

The 14 Year Visa may be considered if the applicant has been resident in the UK for more than 14 years legally or illegally. Again, this will normally qualify the applicant for Indefinite Leave to Remain status as it is considered that he/she considers the UK to be their home. This type of application will be considered as long as there are no strong countering issues, such as a criminal record.

There is also a 7 Year visa. This may be considered if a person has remained in the UK for more than seven years, where that person is facing removal from the UK and he/she has young children with them in the UK who have also resided in the UK for more than seven years.

REGISTRATION AS A BRITISH CITIZEN

Certain persons born between 1961 and 1983 to mothers who were citizens of the UK and its colonies at the time of their birth may apply for registration as a British citizen.

An applicant is entitled to registration if:

- he/she was born after 7 February 1961 but before 1 January 1983, and was born to a mother who was a citizen of the UK and colonies at the time of birth and, had it been possible for women to pass on citizenship of the UK to their children in the same way as men could, would have been a citizen of the UK and its colonies by descent;
- if he/she had been a citizen of the UK and its colonies, would have had the right of abode in the UK and would have become a British citizen on 1 January 1983.

An applicant will meet the second requirement if, at the time of birth:

a)   his/her mother was a citizen of the UK and its colonies either:
- by birth, legal adoption, naturalization or registration in the UK and its colonies; or
- by birth, before 1 January 1949, in a British protectorate, protected state or UK trust territory; or

b)   their mother was, at the time of their birth, a citizen of the UK and its colonies and:

- the applicant was born, or their mother was born, in a British protectorate, protected state, mandated territory or trust territory or in any foreign place in which British subjects came under British extraterritorial jurisdiction; or

- the applicant was born in a non-Commonwealth country and his/her birth was registered, within one year of its occurrence, at a British consulate; or

- the applicant's mother was in Crown service under the UK Government at the time of his/her birth; or

- the applicant was born in a Commonwealth country whose citizenship law had been the subject of an order under section 32(8) of the British Nationality Act 1948, but did not become a citizen of that country at birth.

The third requirement is met if:

- the applicant's mother was, at the time of his/her birth, a citizen of the UK and its colonies by birth, legal adoption, naturalization or registration (except registration on the basis of a marriage on or after 28 October 1971 to a citizen of the UK and its colonies) in the UK, Channel Islands or Isle of Man; or

- one of the applicant's mother's parents (the definition of 'parent' here excludes the father, but includes the mother, of an illegitimate child) was a citizen of the UK and its colonies in the way mentioned above at the time of her birth; or

- the applicant was settled in the UK before 1983 and had, at that time, been ordinarily resident there for five years or more; or

- the applicant is a woman who, before 1 January 1983, was or had been married to a man with the right of abode in the UK.

A successful applicant will become a British citizen by descent. As a British citizen by descent you will not normally be able to pass on British citizenship to any children born outside British territory.

18

Citizenship

There are a number of ways to qualify for British citizenship. The basic requirements for naturalization as a British citizen are as follows. The person who is applying must meet the following requirements. They must:

- be 18 or over;

- not be of unsound mind;

- be of good character;

- have sufficient knowledge of English, Welsh or Scottish Gaelic;*

- intend to have their home (or main home if there is more than one) in the UK. They may, however, live abroad if they plan:

  - to go into or continue in Crown service working directly for the Government of the UK;

  - to work with an international organization of which the UK is a member;

  - to work for a company or association established in the UK;

  - to meet the residential requirements outlined below.

*Since 28 July 2004 all applicants for naturalization are required to demonstrate that they have sufficient knowledge of English. This can be done in two ways:

- by sending a certificate that shows they have attained an ESOL skills for life Entry 3 qualification approved by the Qualifications and Curriculum Authority; or
- by providing a certificate from a designated person showing that they have sufficient knowledge of English.

The three-year residential requirements are that:

- the person applying was in the UK at the beginning of the three-year period that ended on the date the application was received;

- in the three-year period, he or she was not outside the UK for more than 270 days;

- in the last 12 months of that three-year period, he or she was not outside the UK for more than 90 days;

- in the last 12 months of that three-year period, his or her stay in the UK was not subject to any time limit under the immigration laws;

- he or she was not, at any time in that three-year period, in the UK in breach of the immigration laws.

The five-year residential requirements are that:

- the person applying was in the UK at the beginning of the five-year period that ended on the date the application was received;

- in the five-year period, he or she was not outside the UK for more than 450 days;

- in the last 12 months of that five-year period, he or she was not outside the UK for more than 90 days;

- in the last 12 months of that five-year period, his or her stay in the UK was not subject to any time limit under the immigration laws;

- he or she was not, at any time in that five-year period, in the UK in breach of the immigration laws.

PART THREE

EMPLOYERS' SECTION

19

Points-based System and Employers' Registration

APPLYING FOR A SPONSOR'S LICENCE

In November 2008 Tier 2 of the new points-based system (PBS) was introduced as a change to the Work Permit Scheme.

This scheme requires all employers wishing to employ non-UK/EEA nationals to be included on a Sponsors Register.

Registration is open to companies who need to employ non-UK/EEA nationals on the Tier 2 system. There are two aspects of the Tier 2 system: Tier 2 (General) and Tier 2 Intra-Company Transfers (ICT).

Applications for a licence can be made electronically only to the Border Agency (BA).

All applications must be made by the prospective sponsor. A representative may help the prospective sponsor, but may not submit the form on the sponsor's behalf.

After submitting an online application, you are required to submit supporting documentation and the appropriate fee.

Supporting documents

There are certain documents that are required (mandatory documents). The documents required will depend on the status of the company, for instance a limited company, plc or sole trader. Your application will be refused if you do not provide the appropriate mandatory documents.

You must send the original documents or certified copies within ten working days of submitting your online application. A certified copy is one that has been signed by either the issuing authority or by a notary as being an accurate copy of a document.

If you do not provide all the required documents when you make your application the Border Agency will write to you requesting documents. If the documents that are missing are still not provided in the time allowed, your application will be refused.

Where the Border Agency has any doubts about an organization meeting the criteria for the category in which it has paid its fee, further checks may be made, and additional documents to those submitted in support of an organization's application may be requested.

The Border Agency reserves the right to request original documents.

On the application form, the prospective sponsor should indicate under which tiers and categories it wishes to be licensed as a sponsor. Sponsors are licensed to sponsor non-EEA migrants only under those tiers and categories which they indicate on their application. If a Tier 2 sponsor wants to bring in non-EEA migrants under Tier 2 (Intra-Company Transfer), it must apply for a separate licence.

However, employers are currently able to apply for a licence to cover both the Tier 2 General and Intra-Company Transfer categories at the same time. The Border Agency will grant a request to be licensed under a specific tier/category, only if the prospective sponsor meets the licensing criteria for that tier/category.

Payment guidance

Applications for a Sponsor's Licence are subject to a fee. The fee is payable on initial application, or when applying to renew an existing Sponsor's Licence.

Correct completion of the payment details section is very important. Any errors in the payment details could either delay the processing of the application or result in the application being rejected as invalid and returned. It is therefore imperative that you complete the payment details in accordance with the following guidance notes.

How much will it cost?

For Tier 2, there are two categories of licensing fee, depending on the size of the organization. Where a sponsor wishes to become licensed to issue Certificates of Sponsorship under more than one tier, it must pay a multi-tier licensing fee. Arrangements for multi-tier registration will be published shortly before further tiers are launched.

The following fees relate to Tier 2 General and Intra-Company Transfer (ICT) only.

For an organization defined as a small sponsor the licensing fee is £300. For organizations that do not qualify as a small Sponsor, the licensing fee is £1000.

Where an organization has more than one branch and wishes to register each of its branches separately, each individual branch making an application will be subject to the licensing fees stated above. However, an organization that wishes to register its head office and all UK branches together will pay a single licensing fee for Tier 2. Where an organization wishes to register each branch separately, it must pay a licensing fee for each of those branches.

Where a sponsor applies to become licensed under one category of a specific tier, for example tier 2 (General), then later applies to become licensed under a different category of the same tier, for example Tier 2 (ICT), they will not be charged an additional fee for that subsequent application.

Who is considered a small sponsor?

In order to qualify as a small sponsor, an organization that is a company must qualify as a small/medium company in accordance with section 247 of the Companies Act 1985 or, after 6 April 2008, as a small company in accordance with sections 382 and 383 of the Companies Act 2006.

Where an organization is not a company for the purpose of the above sections of the Companies Act 1985/2006 (as applicable), to qualify as a small sponsor, the organization must:

- employ no more than 50 employees;
- have turnover of no more than £5.6 million;
- have a balance sheet of not more than £2.8 million.

Alternatively, an organization can also qualify as a small sponsor if it is a charity.

It is very important to ensure that when making an application under the above regulations, you take into account the most recent amendments to any legislation.

Where the Border Agency has any doubts about an organization meeting the criteria for the category in which it has paid its fee, further checks may be made, and additional documents to those submitted in support of an application may be requested.

How is payment made?

The payment details on the submission sheet must be fully and accurately completed. Payment can be made by cheque or by credit/debit card.

For cheque payments

Cheques should be made payable to The Home Office PBS Sponsorship. All the relevant information must be completed including the account number, the sort code, the cheque number and the amount. Completed cheques must accompany the supporting documents and should be sent to the address stated below within ten working days of submitting the above application.

For credit or debit card payments

Payment details should contain the type of card being used, the amount paid, the name as it appears on the card, the card number, valid from and expiry dates, issue number where available, card verification value (CVV) code, signature and date. The CVV is a three-digit security code which can be found on the back of the card.

Procedure for applications received

The Payment Handling Service will be responsible for considering only the payment aspect of the sponsorship application, and is independent of the Border Agency and does not deal with public callers.

How will the Border Agency consider an application?

When considering a licence application, the BA will ask itself three main questions:

Is the applicant a bona fide organization:

1. Operating lawfully in the UK?

In order to prove this, the prospective Sponsor will need to provide certain documents.

2. Trustworthy?

In order to judge this, the Border Agency will look at the history and background of the organization, its key personnel and those in control of it. Any history of dishonest conduct or immigration crime will be viewed seriously and may well lead to refusal of the application.

3. Capable of carrying out its duties as a sponsor?

The Border Agency will judge this by looking at the organization's processes, and human resources practices to ensure that it will be able to carry out its duties.

Rating

Applications will be rated as follows:

1 – meeting all of the criteria
2 – meeting only some of the criteria
3 – not meeting any of the critera

An **A-rating** will be granted where an organization is marked with a 1 scoring and there is no reason for granting a B-rating or refusing the application.

A **B-rating** will be granted where an organization is marked with a 2 scoring and there are no other reasons for refusing the application.

The application is likely to be refused where an organization is marked with a 3 scoring.

A **B-rating** will not be allowed continuously. You will be expected to supply an action plan which shows what action will be taken to increase your rating to an A – this will be reviewed by a Border Agency Account Manager every three months.

REGISTRATION AS A SINGLE ENTITY OR AS A NUMBER OF BRANCHES

Sponsors who have a number of different offices, branches, locations or campuses (referred to as 'branches' in the rest of this section) will be able to register in a number of ways; for example, seeking a licence as a Head Office and all UK branches or each branch seeking a separate licence.

Alternatively, they can obtain a licence for a group of branches as a single sponsor. For example, a chain store might choose to register all its branches in London as a single sponsor.

Sponsors that have registered branches separately, and subsequently have a licence removed from one of those branches, will not have their licence automatically removed from the other branches.

However, if a number of branches or group of branches of the same organization are individually licensed, and one of those branches has its licence removed or is down-graded to a B-rated sponsor, the Border Agency may wish to investigate other branches of the organization.

If the sponsor is licensed as a 'Head Office and all UK Branches' and has its Licence removed or is down-graded to a B-rated sponsor, then this action will apply to all the sponsor's branches. If the Border Agency removes such a sponsor from the register, then none of its branches will be able to sponsor migrants from outside the EEA. If the sponsor has existing non-EEA migrants, the Border Agency will curtail the leave of the sponsored migrants as they will no longer be working for a licensed sponsor.

Should any sponsor's branches subsequently apply for a licence separately, the BA will take that evidence of previous abuse/non-compliance and the reasons for it into account when considering the application.

CERTIFICATE OF SPONSORSHIP

The system of being issued with a paper work permit no longer exists. If you wish to employ a non-UK/EEA national and have undertaken all required procedures to prove that you were unable to employ a UK/EEA national you are able to issue the applicant with a Certificate of Sponsorship. This is not an actual certificate but a virtual certificate that is allocated a reference number.

Within the licence application you will be asked how many Certificates of Sponsorship you require within each tier you have applied for a licence in. A decision will be made on how many certificates to allocate based on applications made previously and your reasons for requesting these.

KEY PERSONNEL

The sponsor (company) will need to allocate responsibilities to its staff members. There are four roles:

- the Authorising Officer (AO) role;
- the Level 1 User role;
- the Level 2 User role;
- the Key Contact role.

All these roles can be filled by the same person, by four different people, or a combination of 1 to 4 people. All of these people must be based in the UK.

Of these roles, only the Level 1 and Level 2 User roles will have access to the Sponsor Management System as a condition of the role. A person who has access to the Sponsor Management System is a 'User'.

When completing the application form, the AO must decide who within the organization should be a Level 1 User and whether to appoint themselves as the Level 1 User.

The Authorising Officer is responsible for the personnel who use the Sponsor Management System; for example, the number of them, their permissions and their conduct, but it is a Level 1 User who physically sets up their account and gives the users access/permissions. This includes employees of any representatives who have been set up as users of the Sponsor Management System.

The Border Agency will make checks on only the AO, Key Contact and Level 1 User. These will include checks against its own records and against the Police National Computer, or the equivalent in Northern Ireland. If individuals have been convicted of a criminal offence, the BA may refuse the application. If the application is refused because its records show that the AO or named employees have a criminal conviction, this will be explained in the refusal letter. However, the BA will not disclose the specifics of any criminal conviction in that letter.

Authorising Officer

The sponsor will be held fully responsible for the actions of its AO, and so should ensure that it appoints a senior and competent officer from within the organization to this position.

All organizations applying to obtain a licence must appoint an AO and delegate responsibility for their action/duties to that AO. The AO will in turn be held fully accountable for the organization's actions.

The AO must be a permanent member of the sponsor's staff. He or she must not be a contractor, a consultant who is being contracted to undertake a specific project, or an agency member of staff. Where an organization has overseas branches, it can appoint only an AO who is based in the UK branch of the organization.

A sponsor's representative cannot act as its AO. An un-discharged bankrupt cannot act as the AO.

The AO will be responsible for the activities of all users of the Sponsor Management System. This includes both employees of the organization and representatives. Any non-compliance will result in appropriate compliance activity being carried out, which may result in the sponsor losing its licence or being down-graded to a B rating.

The AO role itself does not carry automatic access to the Sponsor Management System. Should the employee in this role require Sponsor Management System access, they will need to be set up as a Level 1 or Level 2 User.

Key Contact

The Key Contact is the person who will act as the main point of contact between the BA and the sponsoring organization. The Key Contact will be the person who will be contacted if there are any queries with the application form, the documents submitted or the payment.

If the AO does not wish to act as the Key Contact, then a person within the organization must be appointed to this position. The Key Contact role has no automatic access to the Sponsor Management System, but again, the person occupying this role can be set up as a Level 1 or Level 2 User if the sponsor wishes.

The Key Contact must be based in the UK. Where an organization has overseas branches, it can appoint only a Key Contact who is based in a UK branch of the organization.

Level 1 User

The Level 1 User will be required to undertake the day-to-day operation of the sponsor's activities through the Sponsor Management System. The Level

1 User will be able to do the following:

- add or remove other users from the Sponsor Management System;

- assign Certificates of Sponsorship to migrants;

- request an increase in the sponsor's limit (that is, in the number of Certificates of Sponsorship it is allowed to issue);

- notify the BAy of minor changes in the sponsor's details (such as a new telephone number);

- complete the sponsor change of circumstances form on the Sponsor Management System, asking the BA to record more significant changes in the sponsor's circumstances;

- report migrant activity to the BA (for example, inform the BA if a migrant goes missing or does not attend his or her job or course).

Only one Level 1 User within the organization may be appointed. If the AO does not wish to have access to the Sponsor Management System, then another person within the organization must be appointed to act as a Level 1 User. The Level 1 User must be based in the UK. Where an organization has overseas branches, the AO can appoint only a Level 1 User who is based in a UK branch of the organization. A Representative may act as the Level 1 User.

Level 2 Users

Depending on the needs of the organization, the sponsor may choose to appoint any number of Level 2 Users. Level 2 Users have a more restricted range of permissions than a Level 1 User. A Level 2 User may:

- assign Certificates of Sponsorship to migrants;

- report migrant activity to the BA; for example, informing the BA if a migrant goes missing or does not attend his or her job or course.

As the AO will be held responsible for the actions of all users, it is advisable to keep the number of users at a manageable level.

Level 2 Users must be based in the UK. Where an organization has overseas branches, the AO can appoint only other users who are based in a UK branch of the organization. A representative may act as a Level 2 User.

Representative

If the sponsor wishes a representative to assist with the issue of Certificate of Sponsorship, it will need to add any of the representative's individual employees who will be dealing with its business to the Sponsor Management System as Level 1 or 2 Users, and set the level of access required. A Representative that is based overseas cannot be added to the Sponsor Management System.

Any representative, who is given access to the Sponsor Management System must either be regulated by the Office of the Immigration Services Commissioner (OISC) (Ambler Collins OISC Registration Number F200100018) or exempt from the requirement to be regulated or otherwise compliant with Section 84 of the Immigration and Asylum Act 1999. It should be noted that anyone compliant with Section 84 through exemption by a ministerial order still has to comply with the OISC code of standards.

Any representative who does not fall within one of these categories or a representative who is not based in the UK cannot act on behalf of the sponsor. If the adviser is not a solicitor, barrister or legal executive, the prospective sponsor should check that they are OISC-authorised or exempt. An adviser could be committing a criminal offence if they act on the prospective sponsor's behalf without being OISC-authorised or exempt. A representative cannot act as the AO.

A representative may not apply for a licence on a sponsor's behalf. A representative may help the prospective sponsor, but may not submit the form on the sponsor's behalf.

A sponsor who is unsure of the status of its representative should contact the OISC, which has a list of authorized advisers.

RESIDENT LABOUR MARKET TEST

Applications made within the Tier 2 (General) Category are usually subject to having to provide evidence that the sponsoring company has attempted to recruit a UK/EEA national by completing a Resident Labour Market Test.

When undertaking the Resident Labour Market Test, the sponsor must always use the advertising methods permitted by the Code of Practice.* The advertisement must include the following information:

- job title;

- main duties and responsibilities of the job;

- location of the job;

- salary package or salary range or terms on offer;

- skills, qualifications and experience required;

- closing date for applications, unless it is part of the organization's rolling recruitment programme; if it is a rolling recruitment programme, the advertisement should show the period of the recruitment programme.

All jobs advertised under the Tier 2 (General) category must be advertised to settled workers in Jobcentre Plus (or in Northern Ireland, JobCentre Online) to pass the Resident Labour Market Test. In addition, the vacancy must also be advertised using one other method permitted by the relevant Code of Practice.*

---

* Code of Practice – The Code of Practice differs for each job listed on the Standard Occupations Classification List.

Each code includes the following:

- the skilled jobs at NVQ or SVQ Level 3 or above in each occupation that sponsors are allowed to issue a Certificate of Sponsorship for;
- the minimum appropriate salary rates;
- the acceptable media and methods for meeting the Resident Labour Market Test.

The only jobs under the Tier 2 (General) category which do not have to be advertised in Jobcentre Plus (or in Northern Ireland, JobCentre Online) are as follows:

- named researchers;

- creative-sector jobs where the Code of Practice states that advertising is not required because:
    - the migrant will be making an additional contribution to the UK labour market
    - the job is the role of director, chief executive or legal partner, where the salary package for the job is £130,000 or above or where there will be stock exchange disclosure requirements.

- the job is on the shortage occupation list; and/or
    - the migrant is switching from Tier 1 (post-study work), the International Graduates Scheme, the Fresh Talent Working in Scotland Scheme or the Science and Engineering Graduates Scheme to continue doing the same job with the same employer under Tier 2 and where he/she has been in that job for at least six months directly prior to switching
    - the migrant has previously qualified as a doctor or dentist
    - is completing their Foundation Programme F2 year in 2009
    - the migrant has current leave to be in the UK as a postgraduate doctor or dentist in further speciality training and he/she needs to apply for further leave under Tier 2 (General) so that he/she can complete that training.

For each recruitment method when the sponsor has undertaken the Resident Labour Market Test, they must keep evidence of this advertising.

SPONSORSHIP MANAGEMENT SYSTEM

The Sponsor Management System (SMS) is a secure IT system that allows licensed sponsors to bring in and manage their migrants under Tier 2 of the points-based system.

Only licensed sponsors have access to the SMS.

As per the information supplied above, there will be different levels of users within your organization.

Only the Level 1 User of licensed sponsors can access the system for the first time. Give the name and details of your Level 1 User when you apply for your licence online. This user can then add further Level 1 and Level 2 Users to the system.

All users will need access to the internet and an email address and must also have Adobe Acrobat Reader to view payment notes.

The SMS is should be used to:

■ manage users and change organization details;

■ view all Certificates of Sponsorship;

■ create and assign Certificates of Sponsorship;

■ comply with sponsorship duties such as reporting migrant activity and withdrawing Certificates of Sponsorship;

■ pay for Certificates of Sponsorship.

COMPLIANCE AND SPONSORSHIP DUTIES

Licensed sponsors are required to undertake certain duties to make sure immigration controls remain effective. The aims of these duties are to:

■ prevent abuse of assessment procedures;

■ capture any patterns of migrant behaviour early which cause concern;

■ address possible weaknesses in processes which cause those patterns;

■ monitor compliance with immigration rules.

The BA has implemented an employer-checking service that offers employers an opportunity to check the status of individuals to work in the UK.

Record keeping

Sponsors are required to keep the following records or documents, and must be able to provide them to BA officials if requested:

- a photocopy or electronic copy of each sponsored migrant's passport or UK immigration status document, showing evidence of their entitlement to work and the expiry date of their permission to stay in the UK;

- each sponsored migrant's contact details (address, telephone number, mobile telephone number), which must be kept up to date.

This is not an exhaustive list.

Reporting

Sponsors must report the following information or events about sponsored migrants to the BA within the time limit given to ensure the continuation of their licence.

The following must all be reported within ten working days:

- if a migrant worker does not attend their first day at work and the reason the migrant gives for non-attendance (for example, a missed flight, illness);

- if a migrant worker is absent from work for more than ten working days;

- if a migrant worker's contract of employment or registration ends (including where they resign or are dismissed), and, if known details of any new employer they have joined;

- if sponsorship ends for any other reason (i.e. if they move into an immigration category that does not need a sponsor or their permission to stay in the UK ends);

- if there are any significant changes in the sponsored migrant's circumstances, (e.g. a change of salary from the level stated on the migrant's Certificate of Sponsorship, other than changes due to annual increments, bonuses or natural progression within the same job, provided this progression is at the same level and is not a promotion since promotions are treated as a change of employment).

■ if the location the migrant is employed at changes;

■ if there are any significant changes in their circumstances, e.g., a change of job or salary (but not a change of job title or an annual pay rise), or a change of the location of employment;

■ if information is obtained which suggests that the migrant is breaching the conditions of his or her leave.

The following must be reported within 28 days:

■ if there are any significant changes in a licensed sponsor's circumstances, e.g. the sponsor ceases trading or becomes insolvent, substantially changes the nature of the business, is involved in a merger or is taken over.

Compliance

Sponsors must comply with the immigration laws and meet the following obligations:

■ ensure that the migrant who is coming to work is legally allowed to do the job, and has the right registration or professional accreditation where needed by law, and keep a copy of the registration document or certificate which can be provided to the BA if requested, e.g. if the migrant is coming to work as a doctor, the sponsor must make sure they have the correct registration to allow them to practise as a doctor in the UK;

■ not employ someone whose immigration status (or lack of) does not allow them to be employed in the position they are applying for, and must stop employing someone who stops being allowed to work for any reason;

■ must assign certificates of sponsorship only to those who, to the best of their knowledge, meet the requirements of the tier or category they are applying under specified in the immigration rules, and who are likely to meet the conditions of their permission to enter or stay in the UK.

Co-operation with the UK Border Agency

Sponsors must co-operate with the UK Border Agency (BA) as follows:

- allow BA staff access to any of their premises on demand (visits may be either pre-arranged or unannounced);

- stick to any sponsorship action plan set by the BA;

- look to minimize the risk of immigration abuse by complying with any good practice guidance that the BA may produce in particular tiers or sectors.

PART FOUR

LIVING IN THE UNITED KINGDOM – PRACTICAL INFORMATION

INTRODUCTION

So you are about to arrive or have arrived to live in the UK. This may be for a short-term work assignment, as the spouse of a UK or EEA citizen, someone who has been sponsored by an employer either as a person with skills in demand or on an intra-company transfer, as a student or someone on the Youth Mobility Scheme.

Where do you start?

What are going to be the issues relevant to you?

How can you prepare and plan for getting your new life started?

Your first contact will be at the point of entry. This may be Heathrow or one of the other international airports, or a seaport. It may be arriving on Eurostar at the St Pancras railway terminal. Wherever it is, there are a number of things that you will need to know and organize to get your life in the UK up and running.

Regardless of your circumstances, the first 24–48 hours are likely to follow a common pattern. You will need to transfer from your arrival point to your initial accommodation. This may be with family or friends, or in a hotel, a bed and breakfast, hostel or some form of student accommodation. Usually eating and sleeping follow in the next few hours.

There will be those whose next consideration will be their first day of work or attending university or college. If you have flown long-haul it is usually sensible to have a couple of days to allow your mind and body become accustomed to the new time zone.

We always advise people, especially those travelling with family, to timetable a couple of free days on arrival to allow them to find their feet. This may include time to find suitable accommodation. Depending on the length of stay, you may want time to get into your new home or, for those with children, a bit of time to settle. For students this may include time to make new friends and to attend induction meetings.

One thing is for sure: this will be a period of change. It is also a period of excitement, especially for those on a first visit to the UK.

There then usually follows a list of common needs.

These may include but are not limited to:

- long-term accommodation;
- getting a mobile phone service provider;
- opening a bank account;
- learning about the public transport systems;
- taking collection of a company car;
- buying your own car;
- finding out about insurance;
- how and from where to get a driver's licence;
- identifying a suitable school for your children;
- looking for employment either part time or full time depending on your circumstances;
- registering with an NHS doctor or dentist;
- what to do in various emergencies;
- help offered by your local authority or council;
- how to register and obtain a National Insurance number;
- what taxes you need to pay and how to apply for tax refunds, if relevant;
- visiting and enjoying the top tourist attractions;
- understanding the protocol, customs and culture of the UK;

- how to get involved in your community, sports clubs and cultural organizations;

- what are bank holidays?

- where is your local church, mosque, temple or religious group?

- how do you access hospitals?

- what are your legal rights and what legal obligations do you have to meet in the UK?

- when do you put out the rubbish and how is it collected?

- do I have to vote?

- where is the best place to do your supermarket shopping and do you need to pay to use a shopping trolley?

- what is an Oyster card and where can it be used?

This list is not exhaustive but does outline the most common issues expats arriving in the UK will have to address.

It is a lot to organize and find out when you have just arrived and for some may seem overwhelming, but rest assured that hundreds of thousands before you have successfully navigated their way through their own personal lists.

Some companies and education providers have well-organized programmes and support systems to help those for whom they are responsible. Some of you may be all on your own and know no one. Sometimes when we are forging new relationships in a new country and culture, it can be the smallest of things that we are too embarrassed to ask. This section is designed to help you with some of these issues.

HAMLET.

20

Employment

If you need to look for employment, finding a job, either full-time or part-time requires a degree of patience and commitment. It is unlikely that you will be able to pick up your ideal job straight away, so ideally you need to begin looking and applying before you leave for the UK.

This is especially relevant to arrivals on the Youth Mobility Scheme or students. Maybe you are the spouse of someone who has come to the UK to work and you want to find part-time employment to make a few social contacts and friends rather than taking on a challenging career position.

WHERE TO FIND WORK

Thinking laterally about how and where to find work could broaden your chances of successfully finding a rewarding and fulfilling job. When searching for employment, it is important to exploit every possible avenue to find the opportunity that will suit you.

Many job vacancies nowadays are handled by recruitment companies, but there are also other ways to find work. Depending on the current stage of your career, all or a combination of the job sources below, could be useful.

Recruitment agencies

Not all recruitment agencies are equal! When deciding which recruitment agencies to register with, there are a few things you should take into account. Always look for an agency that is established and has a good reputation in the marketplace. Good companies are very choosy about the recruitment agencies they align themselves with and will want to work only with recruiters who attract top talent and have proven success. As a result, these agencies will have a much better and wider range of job opportunities on offer and are more likely to help you progress your career.

Another factor to consider is whether the consultants are working on a commission. Many recruitment consultants rely on commission to make up their salary, which can mean that their advice is not always completely objective. It is not unusual for candidates to be talked into taking a job because it is the end of the month and a consultant is down on his or her commission earnings!

Newspapers

Familiarize yourself with those newspapers that cater specifically for your profession and get to know on which days job vacancies are advertised. For example, accountants will use the *Financial Times* and jobs are advertised on Mondays and Thursdays. The *Guardian* advertises media jobs on a Monday. Visit the corresponding online websites to further search for jobs and to research company information. Your local newspaper will also have a 'jobs day' and this should be read weekly too. Again, more senior vacancies tend to be advertized nationally or in industry journals rather than regionally, but your local paper will keep you updated with business information specific to your region.

Avoid regional job magazines which are often merely a tardy repetition of the local paper's jobs pages. Remember that newspapers generally are still a great source for jobs!

Trade magazines/professional journals

If you are a member of a professional body, you should regularly read any relevant magazine, to view advertised vacancies and keep yourself updated with industry information. Many such publications are subscription-only and if you are not doing so already, now is the time to purchase your subscription. Students/graduates embarking on a professional career can often take advantage of reduced subscription rates. These publications are a key source in your job search.

The internet

A key way to search for a job is through the internet. All of the above-mentioned sources, from agencies to newspapers, will have online websites on which vacancies can be found. There are also 'job boards' that range from general jobs, with thousands of job listings, to more specialist sites with fewer jobs. Most sites have search facilities that enable you to specify criteria such as discipline, job type, salary, location. Some provide user logins that will save your details and 'post' any relevant jobs to you as they come in.

One of the largest recruitment companies, Michael Page, carries approximately 10,000 UK-based jobs that you can access online and which are updated hourly, with only current live jobs being advertised (in theory). The online application process is quick and easy, and once you have applied for one job, there is no need to resubmit your CV with subsequent applications. You can also sign up to receive jobs that match your criteria by email. This gives you the advantage of knowing about new job opportunities before other candidates.

Below are some of the most popular online job sites for you to search:

www.totaljobs.com
www.workthing.com
www.scotcareers.co.uk
www.jobsearch.co.uk
www.monster.co.uk
www.michaelpage.co.uk
www.fish4jobs.co.uk
www.jobswales.co.uk
www.hotjobs.yahoo.com
www.jobcentreplus.gov.uk
www.reed.co.uk
www.londonofficejobs.co.uk
www.londonjobs.co.uk
www.topjobs.co.uk/net/HomePage.aspx
www.jobsite.co.uk
www.jobs1.co.uk
www.jobs.nhs.uk
www.mediplacements.com
www.e-cvs.net/top30.asp

One of the quality weekly newspapers in the UK, *The Sunday Times*, runs a special Top 100 companies to work for list once a year. Go to the www.timesonline.co.uk to see who's included on the latest list.

Approaching companies directly

If approached correctly, direct speculative applications can sometimes uncover vacancies. It is sensible to find the relevant recruitment contact within the organization and address any application to them. Do not bombard them with follow-up calls and letters. Take no for an answer and be prepared in some cases not to receive a reply at all, if no vacancy has been advertised. Ensure your cover letter clearly states the type of job you are interested in and ensure it is something you are realistically suitable for!

Many companies these days will have a section on their website that advertises vacancies and gives instructions on how to apply.

On a similar note, do not be afraid to ask friends, colleagues and family whether their employers are recruiting. Many companies today actively encourage employees to introduce prospective candidates to their business, in some cases awarding cash 'bounties' if an individual is sourced and recruited this way.

Job centres

No matter what your opinion is of job centres, they are packed with job vacancies which are updated daily. Advisers are on hand to arrange interviews where appropriate. There are obviously far fewer opportunities advertised via this source for professionals but if you are at the more junior stages of your career, these centres can be helpful.

Intra-company transfer

If you already work for an overseas business with UK offices, you may be able to transfer within your existing company. You will need to speak with your Human Resources or Personnel Department to determine if and how this could be done. For more information please see information regarding Tier 2 (Intra-Company Transfer) on page 95.

APPLYING FOR JOBS

CVs are called a variety of things (e.g. curriculum vitae, resumé). There is no universally-accepted format. The most important attribute of a successful CV is that it clearly explains to the reader what it is that you can do for them. As a quick guide, your CV should be:

- a well-presented selling document;

- a source of interesting, relevant information;

- a script for talking about yourself.

The purpose of your CV is not to get you the job. Its purpose is to get you an interview, and after your interview to remind the person you met with about you. Remember, you are not writing a CV for yourself, you are writing it for the reader. So as you write your CV, put yourself in the shoes of the intended reader.

TEMPORARY EMPLOYMENT

Top tips for temps

As a temp you are an important asset to any hiring company. It is therefore important to do what you can to ensure your success.

Whatever your reason for choosing a temporary contract over permanent work, due to the nature of this type of employment you will be an important asset to any hiring company and to your agency. It is vital for all parties that your assignment as a contractor is successful as quickly as possible.

Temping CV

You may need to tailor your CV for temporary work to ensure your key skills really stand out. If you have completed a number of assignments over a long period of time, check any gaps are accounted for. Your CV should not suggest that you haven't managed to stay anywhere for long! Ensure you can explain each role and your reason for leaving.

Interview

A temporary job may be offered with no prior meeting. Alternatively, an interview for a senior role may be as lengthy as if the role were permanent. If you are called to interview, think about your approach beforehand. You must appear committed to fulfilling your assignment, while not discounting yourself from offers of permanent work. This can be tricky! Each situation is different and generally truthful answers are best, taking care not to concern the interviewer with too much information.

Agencies

Do some research here. Use an agency that seems interested in you and will endeavour to match your job requirements. Try to meet your contact and ensure you understand how they operate. Return calls and emails promptly and keep the agency updated on your availability as requested.

Assignments

Once you have secured an assignment, ensure you have enough details to arrive punctually each day. Pre-check your journey and parking arrangements. Know who you should report to. Be familiar with your standard hours of work and the policy on overtime. Ensure you understand and are familiar with timesheets, paperwork required and pay arrangements. You are expected to honour your assignment for the agreed duration.

Presentation and behaviour

Ensure you are attired suitably for work, whether the dress code is formal or casual. At all times be respectful of company rules. Conduct should be professional, as in a permanent job. Keep personal phone calls and emails to a minimum. Personal internet activity is not acceptable. Do not participate in office politics!

Problems

If you are ill or unable to attend work for any reason, it is vital you inform your agency as early as possible. Failing to do this could seriously jeopardize your assignment. If there are other problems and you are unhappy with your work, again contact your agency quickly and discuss your situation with them.

EMPLOYED OR SELF-EMPLOYED?

The rules about being employed or being self-employed are quite complex. If someone offers you work and gives you a 'choice' of being employed or self-employed or tells you that you are self-employed, don't assume that they know what they are talking about.

The government's local taxation department (the Revenue) can provide all the information and guidance you require about any proposed self-employment, its terms and what agreement or contract you will need.

On the website www.hmrc.gov.uk there is a useful guide to deciding if you could be employed or self-employed. You can find it at 'Low Income' workers.

If you are confident that you are self-employed, the Revenue provides a lot of support for people starting up in business and it is definitely worth visiting the Revenue's site.

If you think you are self-employed you will need to advise your local tax office within three months of your start date.

TIPS ON KEEPING YOUR JOB IN THE UK

- Be flexible – getting your foot in the door is your first step to hopefully becoming indispensable.

- Work hard – working hard and getting noticed can help ensure your job is extended (if temporary) or can lead to a promotion.

- Expect to work long hours – the UK works some of the longest hours in the world, so be prepared to adjust.

- Beat the competition – don't take no for an answer, persist with your enthusiasm to do your job and to do it well.

- Don't whinge, even if others in the office do – it is not recommended. Try to stay positive!

- Don't get involved in office politics!

21

Studying

British qualifications are recognized internationally as being among the very best in the world. They can be gained at all levels, from basic to the most advanced, in a wide variety of subjects and from a wide number of institutions.

STUDENT VISA OVERVIEW

If you wish to study in the UK you should apply to the British High Commission in your country of residence for Entry Clearance.

CONDITIONS OF BEING A STUDENT IN THE UK

The UK Border Agency requires students who wish to study in the UK to meet certain conditions that relate to:

- the place where they wish to study;

- the course selected;

- the ability of the person to follow the course;

- the finances of the person applying;

- the student's intentions during and after the study programme has finished.

The British Government's UK Visas website (www.ukvisas.gov.uk) has full details of visa conditions and should be checked regularly in case there are any changes to the general information supplied above.

FINDING A UK-BASED COURSE TO STUDY

What information should you check about the institution you want to study at?

You must ensure that the institution you wish to study at is listed as a Tier 4 Licensed Sponsor on the Sponsors Register (further information can be found in the Tier 4 section of this book on page 98). You will find details of licensed colleges at: http://www.bia.homeoffice.gov.uk/employers/points/sponsoringmigrants/registerofsponsors/

It is very important that you check the institution you want to attend is in the Register before you make your immigration application. If the institution is not in the Register, your application will be refused and you will have no right of appeal.

The internet is a great place to find out what courses are available in the UK. The British Council website is a particularly good source of information: www.educationuk.org

www.Hotcourses.com and the Universities and Colleges Admissions Systems' (UCAS) www.ucas.com are also websites that can help you search and apply for courses in the UK. Many individual institutions also carry details of their own courses on their own websites.

Once you've found a course that interests you, email, telephone or write to the institution and ask them to send you their prospectus. This is a booklet which provides information on all the courses they run and the facilities they offer. All prospectuses should be free of charge. The British Council's offices outside the UK hold copies of prospectuses from many UK institutions. To find your nearest British Council office, go to www.educationuk.org

Degree courses

There is an official list of institutions that offer recognized UK degrees on the UK Government's Department of Education and Skills website: www.dfes.gov.uk/recognisedukdegrees/ Degree courses can be taken at universities, higher-education colleges, colleges of further education and colleges of art.

Degrees are awarded at two levels – undergraduate or first degree, and postgraduate or higher degree. The most prestigious universities in the UK are Oxford and Cambridge. However, you will need excellent marks or a scholarship to study there.

Applications to universities for undergraduate degree-level courses must be made through a central admissions system called Universities and Colleges Admissions System (UCAS). The UCAS website (www.ucas.com) contains a great deal of information specifically for international students and offers an online application facility.

Vocational and further education

These courses are very popular in the UK and are designed to prepare you for a particular career, give you access to higher education or give you increased skills for a career you are already pursuing. UK qualifications you can attain include: National Vocational Qualifications (NVQs) and Scottish Vocational Qualification (SVQs), Business and Technology Education Council (BTEC) Diplomas and Certificates, City and Guilds awards and Royal Society of Arts (RSA) qualifications.

Professional qualifications

Some professions in the UK require you to take professional qualifications in order for you to practise, e.g. law, medicine and architecture. Many professions in engineering, finance and nursing also have their own professional institutions, e.g. the Institute of Bankers; the Chartered Institute of Marketing; and the Institute of Civil Engineers.

Professional bodies award their own qualifications based on examinations, but rarely will they run their own courses. Courses for such professional qualifications are instead run by colleges and universities, so you'll need to contact your professional body for details about who offers their courses, or search the main search engines, such as Google, Yahoo, etc. to find out the information for yourself online.

Postgraduate courses

If you want to study in London at one of the better private colleges for international students, give Fulham and Chelsea College a look. It is centrally located and offers a range of professional business undergraduate courses that include Human Resources Management, Business Management Travel, Tourism and Hospitality and Marketing. The courses run for one year but you can start them at any time, as they offer a blended learning system. So whenever you want to come to the UK to study you can start one of their courses whatever date you like! Visit www.fccollege.co.uk for more details.

Lots of other postgrad courses are offered throughout the UK. To see a full range of courses, visit the British Council website at www.britishcouncil.org/

Short courses and part-time study

Many part-time courses run throughout the week and/or during the evenings and at weekends. Visit www.floodlight.co.uk for some of those currently available.

FINDING SCHOLARSHIPS

You should contact your local British Council office about any scholarships that are currently available to students from your country who wish to study in the UK. The British Council has representatives in 110 countries and its website provides all the details you need about current scholarships, eligibility, how to apply and how to obtain application forms (most of which are downloadable from the site).

Scholarships administered by the British Council tend to be allocated more than one academic year in advance, so you should start enquiring at least 18 months in advance of your proposed start date.

For your nearest British Council office outside the UK and for more information on scholarships and studying in the UK, visit www.british-council.org/

STUDY METHODS

Although exact methods vary according to the subject you are studying and the institution you are studying at, the structure of most courses falls into either timetabled classes, or a few hours timetabled and the majority of your time working independently. So what learning methods can you expect from a UK course? The following is a general guide from UKCosa (www.ukcosa.org.uk), the UK's Council for International Education:

Lectures

These are large classes, usually lasting around one hour, where a lecturer (or tutor) talks about a subject and the students take notes. On some courses there can be over 100 students at a lecture. There is usually little or no opportunity to ask questions during the lecture. Lectures are usually intended to:

- guide you through the course material by explaining the main points of a topic;

- introduce new topics for further study or debate;

- give the most up-to-date information that may not be included in textbooks.

Seminars

These are smaller classes where students and a tutor discuss a topic. Seminars often last longer than lectures. You will know in advance what the topic is, and the tutor will usually ask some students to prepare a short presentation for discussion. Seminars are usually intended to encourage debate about an issue. This means different opinions will be expressed by the tutor and students. The aim is not for students to be told the 'correct' answer, but to understand the different arguments and make judgements about their merits. This process helps students to learn to analyse a topic critically.

Tutorials

These are meetings between a tutor and an individual student or small group of students. Tutorials are usually intended to give you more focused guidance on:

- a piece of work you are doing;

- a piece of work you have already completed;

- a problem you may be having with a topic or with study methods.

Practical work

On many courses you will have practical workshops, e.g. laboratories on science courses, performance classes in music or drama, a mock trial on a law course. On some courses (e.g. geography) you may go on field trips away from the institution. You may work individually but more usually you will be part of a group. Practical classes are usually intended to give you practical experience of the theories you learn in other classes and to develop practical skills.

Workplace training

On some courses you will have training in a work environment, under the supervision of experienced staff (e.g. working in a hospital on a nursing or medicine course). Other courses offer 'sandwich' placements – an opportunity to spend time away from classes in employment related to your course of study.

Independent study

On any course you will be expected to do some independent study. This usually involves working on your own (or sometimes in a small group with other students) to research a topic and produce written work, or make a presentation at a seminar. This is an integral part of UK academic culture. Independent study is intended to:

- help you develop skills such as critical analysis and problem solving;

- develop your research skills (e.g. finding relevant books and articles);

- allow you to investigate a topic in more detail and develop your own ideas.

Written work

You will almost certainly be asked to produce written work, usually through independent study. Written work may include:

- essays;

- a project or a dissertation (a long essay based on extensive independent research, data collection or experimentation);

- assignment questions (e.g. a series of mathematical problems).

Written work is often assessed. This may be to monitor your progress and identify areas for improvement, or it may contribute to your overall mark or grade for the course.

Other projects and assignments

On some courses you may also be asked to produce work in other forms. For example, you may be asked to write a computer program, prepare a poster presentation about a topic, or prepare practical work for evaluation.

Group work

You may be asked to undertake a piece of work jointly with other students, which may lead to either joint or separate assessment. Group work is designed to encourage team-working skills. If your group includes students from different countries, you may find you have different views from and expectations about how work will be shared and decisions made. Group work can be a good way of learning about working in a multicultural environment.

Examinations and assessments

UK institutions use many different forms of assessment, including:

- 'closed' examinations, where you are not allowed to refer to books or notes and have a specific time to complete a certain number of questions;

- 'open' examinations, where you can refer to books and notes and may even be able to take the question paper away and return it by a certain time;

- assessed essays, individual projects and dissertations;

- group work projects;

- portfolios (a collection of work);

- presentations to a seminar;

- a display or performance of work (e.g. an art show or music performance);

- practical assessments (e.g. in laboratories or on hospital wards).

Some courses are 'continuously assessed', meaning that instead of examinations at the end of the year, your progress is assessed and marked throughout the year.

Plagiarism

Plagiarism means presenting someone else's work as your own. If you present the words or ideas of an author or another student without acknowledging the source, you could be accused of plagiarism. Whenever you use a quotation from a book, or reproduce an author's ideas (even in your own words), you should indicate the source. This process is known as referencing. You may find the accepted ways of quoting and referencing work in the UK are different from those you are used to. Penalties for plagiarism, especially in assessed work and examinations, can be very severe, and may include failing the course. Most academic departments have a preferred style of referencing. *Check with your tutor about how you should reference your work: don't rely on the advice of other students/friends.*

Seeking help

Lecturers and tutors will normally be available to provide help and advice on a very limited basis outside timetabled classes. You should try to ask your questions during tutorials or you may be able to see staff during their 'office hour', a designated time during the week when they are available to see students.

Lecture notes

When you attend lectures, you will need to take notes.

Remember:

- you don't need to write down everything the lecturer says; concentrate on the main points and important details;

- most lecturers use asides (stories to illustrate a point), examples and even jokes; you don't need to write all of these down;

- abbreviations and symbols for common words and terms can help you write faster, but use ones that you will understand later;

- if there is something you don't understand, make a note to ask after the lecture or in a tutorial;

- keep your notes in order in a file; most students 'write up' their notes neatly after a lecture;

- don't just file the notes away until your exams; read through them regularly: this will help with revision;

- if you want to record a lecture on tape, ask the lecturer's permission first.

Don't worry if you find it difficult to understand the lecturer. This will get easier as you get used to their style and, if you are not a native speaker, as your English improves.

Seminar contributions

Seminars can be intimidating if you are not used to this kind of teaching. Don't worry. Many other students feel the same at first. Participating actively in seminars is an important part of the learning process, so try to contribute, even if it seems difficult at first. It is best to do some reading before each seminar, so that you are familiar with the topic and can follow and contribute to the discussion. It may help you to make notes before the seminar of any points you would like to make. If you are having difficulty in seminars, discuss this with your tutor.

Reading

On most courses you will be given a book list. You will not usually be expected to buy or even read every book and journal article on the list. Items on a book list may contain:

- essential, basic reading or reference material for the course;

- an overview of the subject;

- background information;

- useful information for a specific topic or piece of work.

Check with your tutor and other students who are already studying the course which books are essential for you to buy. Most books will be available in your institution's library but essential titles ('core' texts) may be difficult to borrow because everyone on the course needs them. You may be able to reduce the cost of buying books by:

- buying second-hand editions (from students in the later stages of the course, or from a second-hand bookshop), but make sure you buy an up-to-date version;

- forming a group with other students on the course, each buying some of the books and sharing them.

UK ACADEMIC CULTURE

It may take some time for you to adjust to studying in the UK. Academic culture and expectations vary according to the subject, the level of study and the type of institution. However, there are some general trends that you may notice in the UK:

- students often work independently, studying on their own for significant periods of time;

- students are expected to develop critical judgement, which means an ability to assess whether an argument is coherent and well supported by evidence;

- learning large amounts of factual data is important in some subject areas, but in many cases a critical approach is considered more important.

Many UK students will also be going through the process of learning the conventions of academic life. Study skills classes may help you understand what is required. Your tutors should also be able to guide you on how to approach your work.

KNOW WHAT IS REQUIRED

It is important to know what you need to do to fulfil the course requirements. By finding out the answers to some of the following questions, you may be able to plan your work and use your time effectively:

- When writing an essay or assignment, how long should it be?

- Is a piece of work assessed, or is it for 'practice'?

- What proportion of your marks does a piece of work or examination represent?

- How much work will you have to do, and at what stage in the course?

Much of this information may be included in a course handbook: this will be a useful reference throughout the course.

SOURCES OF ADVICE AND HELP

If you have a question or problem with your studies, ask your tutors. They will usually be happy to advise you, or put you in touch with other sources of help. It is best to seek advice early, rather than wait for a problem to become critical.

FEES FOR UK COURSES

Tuition fees and living costs can soon add up. You need to consider the total cost of your course in the UK, including the length of time you will be in the country, the typical amount you need to live on, travel expenses, books, equipment and socialising costs.

Fees can vary and aren't necessarily an indication of the quality of the course. Degree courses range from £5,000 to £10,000 per year. Generally, science courses are more expensive than arts or business courses. All institutions publish course fees on their websites or detials are included in their prospectuses.

ENTRANCE QUALIFICATIONS FOR STUDY IN THE UK

Many countries have their own education and qualification systems. You can check the equivalence of your country's qualifications with those in the UK by contacting the National Academic Information Centre (NARIC) (www.naric.org.uk). Alternatively, the international recruitment staff at the institution where you wish to study may also be able to advise you.

Career-based courses depend on relevant skills or experience. Degree courses require at least three A-Levels or equivalent. For entry to taught postgraduate courses you will need an undergraduate degree or equivalent from your country in a relevant area. For a Doctorate programme (PhD) you will need a UK master's degree or equivalent from your country.

ATTENDING UK INTERVIEWS TO FINALIZE YOUR PLACE ON A UK COURSE

It is very important that you request permission ('leave') to enter the UK as a prospective student rather than as a visitor in order to attend interviews to finalize your study place on a course. You will be expected to provide evidence that you have made contact with UK institutions, e.g. letters inviting you for interview in the UK. Prospective students can stay in the UK for up to six months to make arrangements for their studies. Once you have enrolled at an institution, you will need to extend your stay in the UK as a student. If you have not come to the UK in the immigration category of 'prospective student', you may not be able to do this in the UK and may have to return to your country to make this application.

STUDYING FOR SIX MONTHS OR MORE

If you apply to come to the UK as a student to complete a course of six months or more, you will be given a passport stamp or visa sticker that allows you to work part-time during the term (up to 20 hours per week) and full-time during the vacations. However, for immigration purposes students must be able to show that they can afford to study and live in the UK without having to work.

After you have completed your studies it may be possible for you to stay in the UK for practical training, work experience or full-time employment. The UK government has a scheme called Training and Work Experience Scheme, where employers can apply for permits to employ a person in a particular post for a limited period for work experience or professional training.

The government has also relaxed its policy on students staying on in the UK after studies under the main Work Permit Scheme. Degree-level students, student nurses and postgraduate doctors and dentists in training may be able to stay in the UK for work permit employment if their employer can secure a work permit for them.

It may also be possible to stay on in the UK under the Innovators Scheme and the Highly Skilled Migrant Programme for those who are classed as highly experienced and/or highly qualified students.

Other government schemes have also been introduced, such as the Science and Engineering Graduates Scheme (introduced in October 2004) and the Fresh Talent Scotland Scheme (launched in summer 2005), which may also enable students to remain in the UK to work for a limited period after they successfully complete their studies.

WORK VISAS

You must ensure you have the correct visa to work in the UK. Failure to have a valid working visa or to comply with its conditions may result in deportation. Please see the Immigration section of this book for further information.

BRINGING A DEPENDANT TO THE UK WHILE YOU STUDY

If you are studying for 12 months or more, then your husband/wife/son/ daughter arriving in the UK with you should be given a passport stamp which allows him or her to work. Only your spouse and your children are permitted to come with you to the UK while you study, but your children must be under the ages of 18 years when they first enter the UK. Further information about dependants of international students can be found at www.ukcisa.org.uk

SCHOOLING FOR YOUR CHILDREN WHILE YOU STUDY

If you have brought your children with you, see 'Bringing a dependant to the UK while you study' above. If they are between 5 and 16 years old, they can attend state primary and secondary schools in the UK, as long as they are here as your dependants. You will not have to pay for this. However, some schools may sometimes refuse places to children if they consider their stay in the UK will be too short, or if they have no more places. Further information about dependants of international students can be found at www.ukcisa.org.uk

NEW RIGHTS FOR SAME-SEX PARTNERS

From 5 December 2005, same-sex couples have been able to register a civil partnership and acquire very similar rights and responsibilities to those who are in opposite-sex marriages. This applies to international students who want to enter into a civil partnership in the UK. It also means that international students who have formalized an equivalent legal relationship in another country may be able to bring their same-sex partner to the UK as their dependant, in the same way that students can currently be accompanied by their husband or wife.

HEALTHCARE FOR YOU AND YOUR FAMILY WHILE YOU STUDY

If your course lasts for six months or more, you can receive treatment from the National Health Service (NHS) from the beginning of your stay. You will not have to pay for hospital treatment but you may have to pay for some dental treatment and a standard charge (called a prescription charge) for medicines prescribed by a doctor, although in some cases these charges are waived. The NHS treatment available is also available to your husband or wife and children. As a general rule, children under 16 or under 19 and in full-time education do not normally have to pay for any NHS treatments. To keep up to date with the latest news, go to www.ukcosa.org.uk

STUDENT DISCOUNT CARD

Being a student entitles you to various discounts for shopping, travel, movies and lots more. When you enrol to study in the UK you will be given an International Student Card (ISIC) application form.

Once you've completed the form you will need to attach a passport photograph, have a copy of your enrolment letter from your college and pay a small fee in the form of a cheque (if you have a bank account) or a postal order, which you can obtain from any UK post office. Post the form to ISIC and within about two weeks you should receive your card. For more information about the card, visit www.isiccard.com

LONDON TRANSPORT STUDENT TRAVEL DISCOUNT CARD

If you are based in London, a London Transport student card entitles you to 30% off your travel in London – which includes the underground and the bus network. The application forms are available from the college you've chosen to study at and should be completed in the same way as the ISIC application. You normally receive your card by post within two weeks and you must show you card whenever you purchase your London travel cards in order to obtain a discount.

Other useful student information sites

www.skill.org.uk Skill: National Bureau for Students with Disabilities. Skill operates an information and advice service and works with members and volunteers to promote equality of opportunity for students with disabilities.

www.naric.org.uk UK NARIC: the National Academic Recognition and Information Centre. NARIC advises on the recognition of non-UK qualifications.

www.hero.ac.uk HERO: Higher Education and Research Opportunities in the UK. HERO is the official gateway site to the UK's universities, colleges and research organizations.

www.cisuk.org.uk/ Council for International Students. An organization of and for international students in the UK.

22

Basic Employment Laws

YOUR JOB AND THE LAW

Everyone at work has basic legal rights, and there are new ones on the way thanks both to the Europe Parliament and new laws from the UK Government.

Employment law can be complex and you should always take further advice. Your rights will depend on your own circumstances, so you should always take detailed legal advice on your situation.

YOUR CONTRACT OF EMPLOYMENT

Most employers will give you a written contract of employment as soon as you have accepted a job or on your first day of a new job.

Sometimes you may be given a contract of employment without realizing it. It could be contained in your letter of appointment. It might be called something different, such as a staff handbook. It is not unusual to find a note at the front of a staff handbook saying which sections are parts of the legal contract of employment and which bits simply supply useful information.

Are you an employee or a worker?

Even if your employer does not give you a written contract, some kind of basic contract exists in law as soon as you are paid. But although many people think this is a contract of employment, it may not be so.

This is because you can work for somebody or an organization in two ways. Most people are employees, and should have a contract of employment. It may be for a fixed term, but as an employee you get the legal rights set out below.

The alternative is a 'contract for services'. This is where you are paid to carry out a particular task in return for a fee of some kind. In this situation you are self-employed and do not have rights as an employee. Confusingly, the Inland Revenue use a different definition of self-employed, so you should always be very clear about your position.

TWO KINDS OF EMPLOYMENT RIGHT

You have two kinds of rights at work. The first are those given to you by the law and are called statutory rights. The second are those provided by your contract of employment. They will be different for every job. Normally they will be better than the legal minimum or cover areas where there are no statutory rights. These are called contractual rights. (The only case where a contract of employment can reduce your statutory rights is that employees on fixed-term contracts of more than two years can sign away their right to statutory redundancy pay.)

Both types of employment rights can be enforced in law. Usually this is carried out at an Employment Tribunal. If you think your employer is acting against your contractual rights, take further advice.

YOUR RIGHTS TIMETABLE

Not all employment rights start from your first day at work. Your contract of employment may set out how you get extra or better rights once you have been in your job for a period of time. For example, holiday rights often increase with length of service. The same is true of your statutory rights.

When you apply for a job

You should not be discriminated against in a job-selection process because of your sex, race, disability or because you are a trade union member.

From your first day at work

You should be given a statement showing how much you earn and any deductions that will be made from your pay. (This is not the same as a contract of employment, although a contract of employment can contain this information.)

■ Time off for *maternity leave*, even if you were pregnant when you started the job.

■ *Emergency leave*.

■ Time off for *antenatal care*.

■ *Protection from dismissal on some limited grounds*, including pregnancy, whistle blowing and trade union activity.

■ *Working time rights*.

■ *You have the right not to be discriminated against* for reasons of your sex, including being pregnant, your race or any disability, or for being a member of a trade union.

■ You have a right to *equal pay* with members of the opposite sex doing the same or a comparable job to you.

■ A minimum wage. More information on the minimum wage can be obtained from the government's minimum wage helpline on 0845 845 0360.

■ You are entitled to work in a place which is safe and does not cause you to injure yourself or become ill.

■ You have a right to time off to study if you are 16 or 17 years old.

■ You have a right not to have deductions made from your pay unless you have agreed to them.

■ You have a right to time off for public or trade union duties.

■ You can claim breach of contract if your employer sacks you without giving you the agreed notice, or breaks some other term in your contract of employment.

■ If you are paying National Insurance contributions, you can claim Statutory Sick Pay after you have been off sick for four days in a row.

■ You have a right to be accompanied by your trade union representative or a workplace colleague in a disciplinary or grievance procedure.

After a month

- one week's notice of dismissal;

- payment if you are suspended on medical grounds;

- wages if you are laid off.

After two months

A written statement of your terms of employment which must include your pay, hours, where you are expected to work, holidays and other benefits such as pension entitlement. While the written statement is not a contract of employment, it is very important that you have one, as it can be used if necessary in a court or tribunal if problems arise.

After one year

After one year you are entitled to claim unfair dismissal if your employer sacks you without good reason, or without allowing you to go through a proper dismissal procedure at work. You are also entitled to written reasons for dismissal from your employer. You cannot be made to 'waive' your right to claim unfair dismissal, even if you are on a short-term contract.

You can take up to 13 weeks' unpaid parental leave to care for a child during its first five years. Rights also apply to adopted children and are increased if your child is disabled.

After two years

You can claim statutory redundancy pay if your job has ended and no one has been taken on to do it. The amount depends on your age, your pay and your length of service. You may get more if your contract provides for it.

HOLIDAYS

Most working people aged 16 and over are entitled to at least 5.6 weeks' paid holiday per year. Holidays from work need to be booked in advance and with your employer's agreement.

Your working time rights

People in Britain work longer hours than anywhere else in Europe. However, Europe's working time directive covers most workers and entitles them to:

- 5.6 weeks' paid holiday a year;

- a break when the working day is more than six hours;

- a rest period of 11 hours every working day;

- a rest period of 24 hours once every seven days;

- a ceiling of 48 hours on the maximum average working week;

- a ceiling of an average of eight hours' night work in every 24;

- free health assessment for night workers.

The working time directive is complex, so for more information visit the Department of Trade and Industry's website at http://www.dti.gov.uk/er/index.htm

FAMILY FRIENDLY? RIGHTS FOR PARENTS

New rights for all new parents and better maternity rights are beginning to help make work more family friendly. These include:

- Maternity leave and maternity pay.

- Paternity leave and pay.

- Adoption leave and pay.

- Parental leave. For every child, including adopted children, mums and dads are entitled to take up to 13 weeks' unpaid parental leave before the child's fifth birthday (or the fifth anniversary of the adoption). But it must be taken in blocks of at least a week, and no more than 4 weeks can be taken in any one year. You must give 21 days' notice, and an employer can make you postpone the leave for up to six months, except when you are asking for leave when your child is born or adopted. Many employers will probably be more flexible about some of these conditions. Parents of disabled children can take single days off and leave can be taken up to the child's 18th birthday.

■ Emergency family leave. People are now entitled to unpaid leave for family emergencies when you have to care for a child or other dependant such as an elderly parent in an emergency.

YOUR DISMISSAL RIGHTS

If you have just lost your job, your rights will depend on how long you have worked for your current employer and why you have been sacked. Losing your job is just about the worst thing that can happen to you at work and you should take further advice from your union or other advice agency.

There are three basic ways you can lose your job:

■ through redundancy (this is when your job is no longer required);

■ when you have been dismissed fairly; this will be either because of serious misconduct by you, because you cannot do your job properly or because you do not enjoy legal protection from unfair dismissal;

■ when you have been unfairly dismissed and can take your employer to a tribunal.

What can a tribunal do?

A tribunal can order an employer to give you your job back. However, this is fairly unusual. Usually the tribunal will order your former employer to pay you compensation. The average award is around £3,000.

Treated unfairly?

The law protects everyone at work from being discriminated against because of their race, their sex or a disability. This protection covers pay and conditions, promotion and all treatment at work, including the job interview. There is no legal protection against discrimination on other grounds such as age or because you are gay or lesbian. However, if you are sacked on these grounds and you have worked for the same employer for more than a year, you might be able to claim unfair dismissal.

For further advice, here are some useful contacts:

Citizens Advice Bureau www.citizensadvice.org.uk/
Equal Opportunities Commission www.eoc.org.uk/ for sex discrimination
Commission for Racial Equality www.cre.gov.uk/
Disability Gov UK www.direct.gov.uk/DisabledPeople
LAGER (Lesbian and Gay Employment Rights), call: 020 7704 8066
(lesbians) and 020 7704 6066 (gay men).

HEALTH AND SAFETY

Both employers and employees have rights and responsibilities under health
and safety law:

- your employer has a duty to make sure you are not injured or made ill at
work;

- you have a duty to work safely by co-operating with your employer, and
following safety guidelines;

- your employer has a duty to train you to deal with health and safety issues;

- all workplaces must have an accident book in which work-related injuries
must be recorded;

- your employer must inform and consult you or your union representative
on all health and safety issues;

- you have a right to refuse to do something dangerous if you feel you are in
'imminent and serious danger'.

There are many special regulations about the handling of dangerous
substances or processes and the use of machinery. These normally have to be
displayed or made available to staff. Read them carefully. The Health and
Safety Executive (HSE) enforces and advises on the law. For more
information, visit www.hse.gov.uk or call 0845 345 005.

TAKING A CASE TO AN EMPLOYMENT TRIBUNAL

Employment Tribunals are a special kind of court that deals with employment issues. They are more informal than courts of law. Sometimes lawyers are involved, but in more straightforward cases people will use a union officer, someone from an advice agency or present their own cases.

Costs cannot normally be recovered in Employment Tribunal cases, so if you employ a lawyer you will have to pay their fee out of any damages or compensation you win.

Complaints must be made within three calendar months of the event happening. This is extended to six months for redundancy and equal pay issues. To take a case to an Employment Tribunal you need to fill in a form called an ET1. You can get this from your union, or your local Jobcentre or Unemployment Benefit Office.

Most cases in Employment Tribunals are about unfair dismissal, but other examples have included:

- unauthorised deduction from wages;

- sex, race and disability discrimination;

- equal pay;

- failure to receive the National Minimum Wage.

TRADE UNIONS

Trade unions are organizations that represent people at work. Their purpose is to protect and improve people's pay and conditions of employment. They also campaign for laws and policies which will benefit working people.

Trade unions exist because an individual worker has very little power to influence decisions that are made about his or her job. By joining together with other workers, a great number of people believe there is more chance of having a voice and influence.

The Trades Union Congress (TUC) is affiliated to 70 UK unions representing nearly seven million working people from all walks of life and it campaigns for a fair deal at work and for social justice at home and abroad.

To find out if an employer recognizes a union and/or to find out which union is best to join for your profession, visit the TUC's websites at www.worksmart.org.uk and www.tuc.org.uk and follow the links for 'Unions'.

More advice

The Advisory, Conciliation and Arbitration Service (ACAS) is a public body that promotes good workplace relations. Contact them on 08457 47 47 47 or visit www.acas.org.uk

The TUC operates a 'Know Your Rights' telephone line on 0870 600 4882 (national rate, 8 a.m.–10 p.m.) where you can order information booklets on your employment rights and other workplace issues. It also operates workSMART, where a range of free guides are available helping working people get the best from work (www.worksmart.org.uk). Or visit the TUC's main website at www.tuc.org.uk which is a one-stop shop for the very latest information on workers' rights and latest campaigns.

The information in the Trade Unions section has been reproduced with the kind permission of the TUC and is subject to copyright. © Trades Union Congress 2006.

23

National Insurance
and Taxation

OBTAINING A NATIONAL INSURANCE NUMBER

If you work in the UK you will need to obtain a National Insurance Number, more usually referred to as an NI Number. National Insurance will be deducted from your pay by your employer. This is a form of taxation used by the government to pay for pensions, state benefits (sickness pay, disability allowance, unemployment benefit, etc.) and is used to fund the UK's free National Health Service (NHS), which is one of the best in Europe.

You can obtain a National Insurance Number by contacting the Jobcentre plus NI allocation service helpline on 0845 600 0643. They will make sure you need a number and arrange for you to undertake an 'evidence of identity' interview. When you go for your interview you will generally need to take your passport, a letter from your employer or letters showing you are registered with employment agencies looking for work, and two or three other forms of identification (ID).

Useful contacts

www.dwp.gov.uk/ Department for Work and Pensions
www.jobcentreplus.gov.uk Job centres

The rates of NI you pay vary, so check the rate that applies to you on http://www.hmrc.gov.uk/

For information about what, how and who can receive free services from the NHS, please see www.nhs.uk/ and www.nhsdirect.nhs.uk

TAXATION

As in most countries, the UK requires you to pay tax on your earnings. In the UK there is a staggered taxation system based on the principles of the more you earn the more you pay. The tax year runs from 6 April until 5 April the following year and HM Revenue & Customs (HMRC) is the department responsible for the business of the former Inland Revenue and HM Customs and Excise: www.hmrc.gov.uk/

When you start working in the UK your employer will complete and submit a P46 form to HMRC. Until you receive your tax code from the Revenue you will be taxed at the basic rate of tax – 22%. Once you are issued with a code your tax will be adjusted. If your tax code is not adjusted by the end of the year, you will have to apply to the Revenue to reclaim any tax you consider you've overpaid. Alternatively, if you haven't paid enough tax you will be liable to pay any additional amount of tax due based on your total earnings for the year.

Taxation for company owners

Running your own limited company in the UK is subject to many regulations so always consult the relevant professionals to ensure you have the most up-to-date information and are complying with the appropriate laws. The most useful site for limited company information is www.companieshouse.gov.uk/ or call their helpline on 0870 3333636.

24

Starting a Business

UK LAW

UK legislation changes all the time. Legislation on starting a business going back to the late 1980s is available online from HMSO, where you can also order your own printed copy if you require. Visit www.opsi.gov.uk/ legislation/uk.htm

FORMING YOUR OWN COMPANY

For further information regarding the type of Visas and the regulations about being able to form your own company in the UK, see the Immigration section. Other useful contacts include: www.businesslink.gov. uk and www.companieshouse.gov.uk/

New companies

There are four main types of UK company:

- Private company limited by shares – members' liability is limited to the amount unpaid on shares they hold. This includes those community interest companies (CICs) which are private companies limited by shares.

- Private company limited by guarantee – members' liability is limited to the amount they have agreed to contribute to the company's assets if it is wound up. This includes all RTM (Right to Manage) companies, commonhold associations and those CICs which are companies limited by guarantee.

- Private unlimited company – there is no limit to the members' liability.

- Public limited company (plc) – the company's shares may be offered for sale to the general public and members' liability is limited to the amount unpaid on shares held by them. This also includes community interest public limited companies (that is, CICs which are plcs).

Company incorporation

The Companies Act generally allows one or more persons to form a company for any lawful purpose by subscribing to its memorandum of association. However, a public company or an unlimited company must have at least two subscribers.

Ready-made companies are available from company formation agents whose names and addresses appear in the media or on internet search engines. If you incorporate a company yourself, you will be responsible for filing a range of documents at Companies House, including:

Memorandum of association

This document sets out:

- the company's name;

- where the registered office of the company is situated (in England, Wales or Scotland);

- what it will do (its objects); the object of a company may simply be to carry on business as a general commercial company.

Other clauses to be included in the memorandum depend on the type of company being incorporated.

The company's memorandum delivered to the Registrar must be signed by each subscriber in front of a witness who must attest the signature.

Articles of association

This document sets out the rules for the running of the company's internal affairs. All companies that are limited by guarantee or unlimited, and all CICs (whether limited by shares or by guarantee) must register articles.

In addition, the articles for CICs must comply with the requirements of the

Community Interest Company Regulations 2005. Sample CIC memoranda and articles can be found on the CICs website at www.cicregulator.gov.uk

The company's articles delivered to the Registrar must be signed by each subscriber in front of a witness who must attest the signature.

What is a registered office?

It is the address of a company to which Companies House letters and reminders will be sent. The registered office can be anywhere in England and Wales (or Scotland if your company is registered there). The registered office must always be an effective address for delivering documents to the company, and to avoid delays it is important that all correspondence sent to this address is dealt with promptly. If a company changes its registered office address after incorporation, the new address must be notified to Companies House.

What is the minimum number of officers a company requires?

Every company must have formally-appointed company officers at all times.

A private company must have at least:

- one director – but the company's articles of association may require more than one;

- one secretary – formal qualifications are not required. A company's sole director cannot also be the company secretary.

A public company must have at least:

- two directors;

- one secretary – formally qualified.

All company officers have wide responsibilities in law.

Can anyone be a company director?

In general terms, yes, but there are some rules. You can't be a company director if:

- you are an undischarged bankrupt or have been disqualified by a court from holding a directorship, unless given leave to act in respect of a particular company or companies;

- in the case of plcs or their subsidiaries, you are over 70 years of age or reach 70 years of age while in office, unless you are appointed or reappointed by resolution of the company in general meeting of which special notice has been given.

There is no minimum age limit in the Companies Act for a director to be appointed in England and Wales. However, he or she must be able to consent to their own appointment. You should seek legal advice if you intend to have a very young person as a director of your company.

In Scotland the Registrar will not register for any company the appointment of a director under the age of 16 years old. A child below that age does not have the legal capacity to accept a directorship, as outlined in the Age of Legal Capacity (Scotland) Act 1991.

Some people not of British nationality are restricted as to what work they may do while in this country. If you need more information about whether such a person can become a director of a UK-registered company, contact the Home Office Immigration and Nationality Department on 0870 606 7766.

Can I choose any name I want for my company?

No. There are some restrictions on your choice of company name. It is important to check that the name you want is acceptable to Companies House before you complete the company formation documents.

Briefly, the restrictions are that:

- you cannot register the same name as another company;

- the use of certain words is restricted;

- names likely to cause offence are not allowed.

It is also important to check if your chosen name is similar to any other names already on the register. If your chosen name is too like another name, an objection could be made within the 12 months following the incorporation of your company and you could be directed by the Secretary of State to change the company's name.

Names cannot be reserved and formation applications are not processed strictly in order of time or date of receipt. In the unlikely event that Companies House receive more than one application to register the same name, only one will be registered. The second will be refused because the name would then already be on the names index. There can be no guarantee which application will be processed first. In general, company incorporation applications delivered electronically are processed more quickly than other applications delivered on paper.

How much does Companies House charge to incorporate a company?

The standard registration fee is £20, but a premium service (£50) provides incorporation on the day it receives the formation documents. There is an additional fee of £15 to be paid to the Regulator when forming a CIC. For users of the electronic filing service, the standard fee is £15 and the premium same-day service is £30. To be able to incorporate electronically, you must either purchase suitable software or develop your own software. Visit www.companieshouse.gov.uk/ for more information.

Where can I obtain forms to incorporate a company?

The forms are available free of charge from Companies House. Specimens of these documents can be obtained from legal stationers, accountants, solicitors or company formation agents. Community interest statements and excluded company declarations (only relevant for CICs) can be obtained from the CICs website.

PUBLIC LIMITED COMPANIES

What is a public limited company?

■ Company documentation must state that it is a public limited company both in its memorandum and in its name. The memorandum must contain a clause stating that it is a public limited company and the name must end with 'Public Limited Company' or 'plc' (or, if it is a Welsh company, the Welsh equivalents 'Cwmni Cyfyngedig Cyhoeddus' or 'CCC').

■ For public limited companies that are also CICs, the name must end with 'community interest public limited company' or 'community interest plc' (or, if it is a Welsh company, the Welsh equivalents 'cwmni buddiant cymunedol cyhoeddus cyfyngedig' or 'cwmni buddiant cymunedol ccc').

■ The memorandum must be in the form specified.

■ It must have an authorized share capital of at least £50,000.

■ Before it can start business, it must have allotted shares to the value of at least £50,000. A quarter of them, £12,500, must be paid up. Each allotted share must be paid up to at least one quarter of its nominal value together with the whole of any premium.

Can a plc issue shares in another currency?

Yes, if it has passed the necessary resolutions to adopt that currency as part of its authorized capital and given the directors the authority to allot that capital. However, it must always have at least the authorized minimum of £50,000 sterling in issued capital, irrespective of what other currency it uses.

A company may use as many currencies as it wishes for its share capital provided that they are true currencies.

When can a plc start business?

A newly-formed plc must not begin business or exercise any borrowing powers until it has a certificate issued under section 117 of the Companies Act 1985 confirming that the company has issued share capital of at least the statutory minimum (see the first question). Once issued, the certificate is proof that the company is entitled to do business and to borrow.

Do these rules apply to an overseas plc?

Most of the above rules do not apply to a public company formed abroad. On establishing a branch or place of business in Great Britain, such a company is governed by Part XXIII of the Companies Act 1985, just as any other overseas company is. However, besides Part XXIII of the Act, the Company is also governed by regulations in its country of incorporation, by certain parts of the Financial Services and Markets Act 2000, and by the City Code on Takeovers and Mergers.

DETAILS TO BE SHOWN ON COMPANY STATIONERY

Under the Companies Act 1985 your company must state its name (as it appears in its memorandum of association) in certain places and on its business stationery. Your company must also give certain information on all its business letters and order forms.

Every company must paint or affix its name on the outside of every office or place in which its business is carried on – even if it is a director's home. The name must be kept painted or affixed and it must be both conspicuous and legible.

The company must state its name, in legible lettering, on the following:

- all the company's business letters;

- all its notices and other official publications;

- all bills of exchange, promissory notes, endorsements, cheques and orders for money or goods purporting to be signed by, or on behalf of, the company;

- all its bills of parcels, invoices, receipts and letters of credit.

It must also show on all its business letters and order forms its place of registration and its registered number. The place of registration must be one of the following, as appropriate:

For companies registered in England and Wales:	*For companies registered in Scotland:*
Registered in Cardiff	Registered in Scotland
Registered in England and Wales	Registered in Edinburgh
Registered in England	Registered in London
Registered in Wales	

A company incorporated outside Great Britain which opens a branch or place of business in Great Britain must be registered and must give similar details to those stated in this chapter.

Community interest companies (CICs)

For further guidance see the CICs website at www.cicregulator.gov.uk

ONCE YOU'RE UP AND RUNNING

The first accounts of a *private company* must be delivered:

■ within ten months of the end of the accounting reference period; or

■ if the accounting reference period is more than 12 months, within 22 months of the date of incorporation, or three months from the end of the accounting reference period, whichever is longer.

The first accounts of a *public limited company* (plc) must be delivered:

■ within seven months of the end of the accounting reference period; or

■ if the accounting reference period is more than 12 months, within 19 months of the date of incorporation, or three months from the end of the accounting reference period, whichever is longer.

What else must I tell Companies House?

Here are some of the important things that you must tell Companies House, using, in most cases, a special indexed form that it provides on its website, and within the time limits stated.

■ Changes of director(s) and secretary, within 14 days. For:

Appointments	use Form 288a
Resignations	use Form 288b
Change of personal details	use Form 288c

- *Details of new shares being allotted,* within one month. Use Form 88(2).

- *Any special or extraordinary resolutions and certain types of ordinary resolution,* within 15 days of them being passed by the company. There is no special form but Companies House needs to receive a copy of the resolution.

- When a resolution alters the memorandum or articles of association of a company, a copy of the amended document must also be sent in at the same time as the resolution.

- *Details of any mortgage or charge created by the company,* within 21 days.

- *A change of registered office,* within 14 days. Use Form 287. The change becomes legally effective only when Companies House has registered the form.

- *An annual return Form 363s* to Companies House at least once every 12 months. The company has 28 days from the date to which the return is made up to do this.

Filing the right forms on time is a legal requirement. If your accounts are delivered late, there is an automatic penalty. This is between £100 and £1,000 for a private company and between £500 and £5,000 for a plc.

In addition, directors may be prosecuted for not filing certain documents. If convicted, they will have a criminal record and be liable for a fine of up to £5,000 for each offence. In some cases, they could also be disqualified from being a company director or taking part in the management of a company for up to five years.

Further information

Companies House Contact Centre staff normally provide an immediate answer to your query, but if they are unable to provide an answer they will transfer you to someone who can. You can get in touch with the

Companies House Contact Centre on 0870 33 33 636, or by email at enquiries@companies-house.gov.uk. Lines are open 08.30–18.00 UK time Monday to Friday, except national holidays.

VAT: THE BASICS

Value Added Tax, or VAT, is a tax that applies to most business transactions involving the transfer of goods or services. At the time of print the current VAT is 17.5%.

VAT is a tax on consumer expenditure. It is collected on business transactions, imports and acquisitions. And as most business transactions involve supplies of goods or services, VAT is payable if they are supplies made in the UK or the Isle of Man by a taxable person in the course of a business and are not specifically exempted or zero-rated.

There are three rates of VAT:

■ a standard rate, currently 17.5%;

■ a reduced rate, currently 5%;

■ a zero rate.

Some supplies are exempt from VAT, which means that no VAT is payable. Also, supplies are outside the scope of VAT if they are made outside the UK and Isle of Man or not made in the course of business.

REGISTERING AND CHARGING VAT

The supply of any goods and services which are subject to VAT at any rate are called taxable supplies, whether you are VAT-registered or not.

If the value of your taxable supplies is over a specific limit, you need to register for VAT, unless your supplies are wholly or mainly zero-rated, in which case you may apply for exemption from registration.

You may be charged a penalty if you register late, and as the easiest way to register for VAT is by using the online Registration service, you need to go to the website and make sure you are complying with the necessary guidelines. Visit: customs.hmrc.gov.uk/channelsPortalWebApp/channelsPortal WebApp.portal?nfpb=true&_pageLabel=pageVAT_Home

AFTER REGISTRATION

You need to charge VAT on all your taxable supplies from your date of registration and keep:

- a record of all standard-rated goods and services you supply or receive as part of your business;

- a separate record of any exempt supplies you make;

- a VAT account.

At pre-set intervals you need to fill in a VAT return with details of your sales and purchases. You can do this online or by using a paper return. If the VAT on your sales is more than the VAT on your purchases, you pay the difference. On the other hand, if the VAT on your purchases is more than the VAT on your sales, you can claim the difference.

For small businesses, there is a flat-rate scheme that simplifies VAT accounting procedures to save time and money.

25

Childcare, Schools and Education

CHOOSING CHILDCARE

If you're considering childcare you have a number of options. These include:

- crèches – provide occasional care for children under eight;

- toddler groups – informal groups of parents and carers that meet locally with their children on a regular basis, usually including children who are under five;

- pre-schools and playgroups – provide play-time and often early education to under fives;

- day nurseries – provide care for children from birth to four or five and beyond, often integrated with early education and other services;

- out-of-school or 'kids' clubs – offer children aged four to 12 a safe and stimulating environment in which they can play and learn outside school hours;

- childminders – usually look after children under 12 in the childminder's own home and often collect school-aged children from a nearby school;

- home childcarers – registered childminders who work in your own home (your home will need to be registered as a childcare setting if you use a home childcarer);

- nannies – provide childcare in your own home and can look after children of any age.

FINDING CHILDCARE

Finding suitable childcare can be difficult but the following can help you make the right option to suit your own circumstances.

■ The Childcarelink website offers comprehensive information and advice about childcare and lets you search for childcare by postcode, town and clickable map area. Visit www.direct.gov.uk

■ Your local Children's Information Service (CIS) can advise you on childcare options and availability in your area. You can get the telephone number of your nearest CIS by calling Childcarelink on freephone 0800 096 0296 or visit www.childcarelink.gov.uk/index.asp

ENSURING CHILDCARE QUALITY

Entrusting a stranger with your child is a big step, so before you choose childcare you should do some research. Here are some suggested options:

■ *Ofsted registration* – All childminders and day-care providers, including playgroups, pre-schools, private nurseries, crèches and out-of-school clubs for under-eights, must be registered by Ofsted (The Office for Standards in Education). Ofsted registers these providers and makes sure they meet the national standards for under-eights daycare and childminding, and ensures that all those who work with children are fit to do so. Ofsted also checks that the environment provided for children is secure and safe.

■ *Childcarelink* – You can check if a childcare provider is registered by asking to see a registration certificate. If you have any doubts about a provider, check with your local CIS. You can get the telephone number of your nearest CIS by calling Childcarelink on 0800 096 0296 or visit www.childcarelink.gov.uk/index.asp

■ *Ofsted inspection reports* – These reports provide detailed information on individual childcare providers (except for childminders), based on Ofsted's annual inspections. Visit www.ofsted.gov.uk/ and search for 'Inspection reports' using your own postcode.

■ *Do your own research* – It is always a good idea to visit childcare providers yourself. Inspections and accreditation are no substitute for your own judgement. When you do visit, ask plenty of questions. If you're thinking of employing a nanny, bear in mind that government-sponsored registration and accreditation schemes do not apply to them. It is up to you, as parent and employer, to make sure that you hire a nanny who will look after your children well.

REPORTING CHILDCARE CONCERNS AND COMPLAINTS

If you have a concern or complaint you can't resolve with your registered childcare provider, although Ofsted does not usually become involved in complaints over fees and contractual arrangements, you can call Ofsted's Early Years Complaints helpline on 0845 601 47 72.

HELP WITH CHILDCARE COSTS

Childcare can be expensive, so it's worth checking to see if you qualify for any help. But be aware that all government programmes that provide help with childcare costs require you to use Ofsted registered childcare. Visit www.direct.gov.uk

FREE EARLY YEARS EDUCATION FOR THREE AND FOUR YEAR OLDS

If your child is three or four, they are entitled to free early years education at a registered provider. This includes five sessions a week, two and a half hours per day, for three terms each year. Your local CIS can advise you on availability in your area. You can get the number of your nearest CIS by calling 0800 096 0296 or visit www.childcarelink.gov.uk/index.asp

OVERVIEW OF THE EDUCATION SYSTEM

There are different types of school and methods of application when choosing a school for your child. As a UK citizen your child is entitled to a free education up to the age of 16 years (compulsory school age), or to the age of 18 years with added sixth-form education. UK schools will welcome your children, whatever their faith or nationality. Multi-faith assemblies in primary and secondary schools are commonplace and children are taught to respect each other's beliefs.

Primary schools

Your child's first day at 'real school' is a big step, and from now on their life outside home will develop daily. New experiences will help your child grow and become independent, underpinned by your own active support.

These years are crucial for reading, the one skill which children need to access the rest of their education successfully. The importance of reading outside school is continually being stressed by educationalists and psychologists. In the UK, guidance is available for child development, and there are some useful tips on the government's website at www.direct.gov. uk/EducationAndLearning

PREPARING YOUR CHILD FOR SCHOOL LIFE

If children have a good idea of what school is going to be like and have practised the skills needed there, they're less likely to find the experience stressful. You can build your child's confidence by taking a positive approach:

- explain where they'll be going and for how long;

- answer questions, and iron out wrong impressions by asking what they think school might be like;

- turn-taking games and little role-plays at home can help your child get into the right frame of mind;

- practise the practical things, such as coping with coats and shoes, and opening lunchbox items like yoghurts and drinks;

- don't dismiss your child's fears – things that are obvious or silly to grown-ups can seem like terrible obstacles to a five-year-old.

WHAT YOUR CHILD WILL LEARN

The first two years of primary school are called Key Stage 1, and the next four are Key Stage 2. For each of these stages, the government has put in place a teaching framework called the National Curriculum which lays down the subjects taught at every school. For more information on the National Curriculum, see below.

Homework

All schools have their own homework policies, and you can request a copy so you can see what your child should be doing. Some schools make sure parents are aware of homework by asking them to sign a homework book.

Out-of-school arrangements

Breakfast clubs and after-school clubs are available at many schools and offer parents or carers the chance to drop children off and collect them outside ordinary school hours. Individual schools or the ChildcareLink freephone service on 0800 096 0296 can give you more information, or visit www.childcarelink.gov.uk/index.asp

Home education

In the UK, parents do not have to send their children to school, but the law does require that children are educated.

Successful schools

Since 1994/5, the UK Government has measured schools' performance through annual inspections and the publishing of an annual report which shows, every year, which schools have achieved 'successful school' status.

Up to and including 2003/4, some 2,669 schools and 65 colleges have been identified as particularly successful.

Schools are considered 'successful' on the basis of:

- the judgements in the school's inspection report, in particular those relating to overall effectiveness, (since January 2000), the quality of teaching, leadership and management, and improvement since the last inspection;

- the attainment of the school's pupils in national tests and exams. In both cases the selection takes into account the particular circumstances of schools.

Colleges should be very well led and provide a consistently high standard of education and training for their students.

For more information, visit www.ofsted.gov.uk/ and select the 'successful schools' link.

UNDERSTANDING THE NATIONAL CURRICULUM FOR ENGLAND

The National Curriculum sets out the stages and core subjects your child will be taught throughout their school life. Children aged five to 16 in state or maintained schools must be taught according to the National Curriculum. Knowing the stages and subjects that make up the National Curriculum is important.

National Curriculum subjects

The National Curriculum, taught to all pupils, is made up of modules, known as Key Stages. It is organized on the basis of four key stages, as shown below:

	Key Stage 1	Key Stage 2	Key Stage 3	Key Stage 4	
Age	5–7	7–11	11–14	14–16	
Year groups	1–2	3–6	7–9	10–11	
English	■	■	■	■	National
Mathematics	■	■	■	●	Curriculum
Science	■	■	■	●	core
Design and Technology	■	■	■	●	
Information and Communication Technology	■	■	■	■	National
History	■	■	■		Curriculum
Geography	■	■	■		non-core
Modern Foreign Languages			■	●	foundation
Art and Design	■	■	■		subjects
Music	■	■	■		
Physical Education	■	■	■	●	
Citizenship			▶	▶	

■	Statutory from August 2000
●	Statutory from August 2001
▶	Statutory from August 2002

Schools don't have to use these titles for subjects, and some subjects can also be taught together under one name, as long as the National Curriculum is covered. If you want to know more about the National Curriculum for England visit: www.nc.uk.net

Teachers assess children against the National Curriculum levels regularly as they learn. You'll receive information about the level your child has reached at parent–teacher evenings and in their school reports.

THE NATIONAL CURRICULUM KEY STAGE TESTS

At the end of each Key Stage there are national tests. Children can't 'fail' these tests. They are intended to show if a child is working above or below the target levels for their age, so that the right plans can be made for their future learning. They also allow schools to see whether they are teaching effectively, by looking at their pupils' performance against national results.

Key Stage 1 tests for seven-year-olds have two elements, teacher assessment and written tests in reading, writing (including handwriting), spelling and maths. The tests are spread out, and altogether they last for less than three hours.

Key Stage 2 tests for 11 year-olds also comprise teacher assessment and written elements. The written tests cover:

- English – reading, writing (including handwriting) and spelling;

- Mathematics (including mental arithmetic);

- Science.

These tests are held in mid-May, and altogether they last less than five-and-a-half hours.

CHOOSING A SCHOOL

State schools

These schools are funded entirely from government money and are found in all towns. They are open to all children regardless of race, religion or beliefs. There are different kinds of state school:

- community schools provided by the local authority which is responsible for admissions;

- foundation schools provided by a foundation or trust and for which the governing body is responsible for admissions;

- voluntary schools provided by a foundation or trust; most voluntary schools have a religious character and are known as faith schools.

If you have a firm faith, you may find a faith school that you would like your child to attend. It may be farther away from your home but the local authority may be able to help with travel. If the school is voluntary aided, you will need to approach the school directly about its admissions criteria. For voluntary controlled faith schools the local authority is responsible for admissions.

Independent (private) schools

Parents may choose to pay for their child's education at an independent school. These schools are funded privately. Parents usually pay fees annually in advance and are expected to be able to pay for the duration of the secondary school (i.e. for the whole four years). Rates vary so it's best to talk to the school directly about their fees.

SCHOOL UNIFORM

The governing body of each school decides on the uniform policy or dress code, and it is the headteacher's responsibility to make sure pupils keep to the rules. If you have any complaints about the uniform policy or dress code, talk to the school's governing body.

Cost of school uniform

When deciding on a uniform policy, all schools are expected to consider cost. No school uniform should be so expensive as to leave pupils or their families feeling excluded.

The government believes it is unacceptable for the cost of a uniform to stop parents from sending their child to the school of their choice. Governing bodies should consult parents for their views and concerns before changing or deciding on a new uniform policy.

Physical education (PE)

School uniform often includes clothing required for PE lessons. Schools are supposed to choose a PE kit which is practical, comfortable and appropriate to the activity involved. Sex and race discrimination issues must also be considered. As with the regular school uniform, school governing bodies are expected to consider the cost to parents when deciding on a policy for PE kit.

Breaching uniform policy

If your child breaks the rules when it comes to school uniform, they could be punished by the headteacher. More serious punishments like suspension or expulsion from the school are considered acceptable only if the pupil's behaviour has been generally defiant in other areas as well.

Schools should be considerate if a pupil does not keep to the uniform policy, and try to find out why it is happening. If a family is having financial difficulties, the school should allow for this and give the parents time to buy the right items.

Cultural, race and religious requirements

While pupils must stick to the school's uniform policy, UK schools must be considerate to the needs of different cultures, races and religions.

Sex discrimination issues

Schools should ensure that their uniform policy does not discriminate on the grounds of gender. For example, girls should normally be allowed to wear trousers. Uniform rules should not disadvantage one gender compared with the other.

SCHOOL TERM DATES AND HOLIDAYS

The dates for school terms and holidays are decided by the local authority (LA) or the governing body of a school. Some LAs have introduced a year with six terms, each of similar length. However, for the majority of schools the current school year is divided into three terms. To locate your LA, go to www.dfes.gov.uk/leagateway/index.cfm?action=address.default

Holidays during school term-time

You should not normally take your child on holiday in term-time as it can be disruptive both to your child's education and to the school.

Holidays in term-time can be sanctioned only by the headteacher or someone with appropriate authority. They can agree to more than ten school days' absence in any school year only in exceptional circumstances. You should discuss proposed holidays with the school before you book them.

Each holiday request will be treated individually and the following will be taken into consideration:

■ the time of year for the proposed trip;

■ if it's near any exam dates;

■ your child's overall attendance pattern;

■ any holidays already taken in the school year;

■ the age and stage of education of your child;

■ your wishes.

COLLEGES AND UNIVERSITIES

Universities and colleges in the UK are increasingly international. When you study here, you are likely to find yourself meeting students from all over the world. More than 90 countries may be represented on campus and each student makes a unique contribution to the life of the institution, both academically and culturally.

This internationalism is demonstrated by student societies established within the Student Union, where those centred on religious or geographical themes are numerous.

Colleges and universities make an effort to meet international students' dietary and religious needs. Vegetarian dishes are served daily in university canteens. Single-sex accommodation is usually available on campus on request. Universities pride themselves on giving students the freedom to worship and practise their religion; prayer areas and chapels for all the major religions of the world are easily accessible.

If you are staying in private accommodation, you should tell your hosts of any customs that you wish them to respect while you are staying with them. For example, if there are certain foods that you may not eat or if you need some privacy every day to pray or meditate, explain these needs to your hosts and ask for their co-operation.

Studying in the UK

If you are moving to the UK and have finished school, you will find some useful information on further education, including postgraduate study in other parts of this book, so refer to the Contents.

Relevant websites

http://www.aimhigher.ac.uk/universities_colleges_hei/index.cfm
Allows you to view institutions in specific areas across the UK. Also offers advice about student financing and how to apply.

www.direct.gov.uk/EducationAndLearning/UniversityAndHigherEducation/
How to apply for a college or university placement once you've qualified from a UK school.

26

Housing

BACKPACKER AND STUDENT HOUSING IN LONDON

Unless you have mates, or mates of mates, to crash or 'doss' with, you will need to look at short-term accommodation until you get established.

If your main goal is to start a job in the UK quickly after you arrive, you should plan to find a short-term, well-located, reasonably-priced, safe and secure place to stay. There are lots of accommodation options and some types are far more suitable than others.

- **Backpacker hostels in London** Traditionally the way to get backpacker accommodation in London is through a hostel. They are relatively inexpensive and a great way to meet lots of travellers, like-minded or not. Cleanliness and comfort and privacy levels vary between the different London hostels, so it pays to shop around. Visit www.workgateways.com for a list of hostels. Also see www.tntmag.co.uk/ and www.gumtree.com

- **Guesthouse, small hotel or Bed & Breakfast** For the working traveller, in terms of privacy and a safe place for your belongings, you may want to consider the above rather than a hostel. In most guesthouses or small hotels you will probably have your own room. However, you may have to share a bathroom with several other guests. If you can share a twin room with a mate, you will find it even cheaper. Safes for your valuables are sometimes provided. Hot breakfasts are usually included and you'll have a cupboard in which to hang your job-searching suit! If you go out of peak season or decide to stay longer term, many UK guesthouses and small hotels will offer a discount to you if you ask.

- **Shared accommodation** Visit www.accommodationlondon.net and you will find a range of studio apartments and shared houses in London which are fully equipped and accessible. They are usually in demand so you need act quickly.

- **Live-in accommodation in the UK** Many jobs within a pub or hotel environment, such as waiting tables, bartending, reception and chef jobs, provide live-in work arrangements. Often in a live-in arrangement some meals and board are included, and depending on the number of hours you work you can be paid wages on top of this. Live-in work is more often found outside London, in regional UK areas, smaller cities and towns.

TYPES OF LONGER-TERM ACCOMMODATION

- **Flats** are generally apartments with one to three or more bedrooms which are to be let, or rented, as an entire unit.

- **Flat-shares** come available when a flat is already occupied and one or more bedrooms become available for rent. This means you'll be sharing common facilities of the flat such as kitchen, lounge and usually bathroom.

- **Bedsits** are popular in the UK. Usually an old multilevel house will be split up into mini-apartments. Each mini-apartment will generally be a bedroom with perhaps some room for a sitting area; sometimes there are sinks in the bedrooms as well. Bathroom and kitchen facilities are generally shared with either all those in the house, or just tenants on the same floor. This can be an inexpensive and convenient accommodation option. A bedsit is a kind of hybrid between a guesthouse and renting a flat.

- **Houses** can be rented but are harder to find and extremely expensive in London. They are more easily found in regional UK areas.

BEFORE RENTING IN THE UK: ADDITIONAL COSTS AND CONSIDERATIONS

- **Location** Different boroughs (suburbs or neighbourhoods) in London and the UK have a different lifestyle and price associated with them. So research your chosen location well before you move, so you know what to expect.

- **Transportation links** Before signing a lease anywhere, you should be sure to walk to the nearest transportation links, catch the bus, train or tube at rush hour and see how long it takes you to get to other key areas. In general walking proximity to a Tube or British Rail station is highly sought after. A bus stop nearby is the next best thing.

- **Furnishings** Most UK flats and homes are rented furnished, with basics. If a flat is advertised as furnished, be sure you determine exactly what is provided. If something is in a particularly poor state, ask to have it replaced. It is the landlord's responsibility to provide the basics, in good repair, in a furnished flat.

- **Bond** Most, if not all, rental arrangements will require you to pay a bond, which is usually equivalent to a full month's rent. You will usually get this bond back after you have moved out and the accommodation has been inspected.

- **Estate or letting agencies** Unless you find flat-shares through friends, or magazines and websites, most of the ads for flat rentals in the newspaper are through estate or letting agents. Agents have shops across the UK and they should be able to offer you advice, ideas and information on what they have available. Some agents have better reputations than others, but as long as you ask questions and read your lease very carefully you should have a good experience.

- **Flat mates** Can make living affordable and fun. Often people at your work will know someone with a room available. In general you should not have a problem finding an affordable location. One word of advice: if you are signing a lease for a three-bedroom flat, you should try to be sure that you have three people ready to move in who are planning to stay for the duration of the lease. Assuming you will always be able to find someone suitable to fill up the flat can lead to headaches and financial distress!

- **Council Tax** is a compulsory tax levied by the local government or borough council and is paid by all residents of that borough or neighbourhood. When you sign a lease and rent a flat, be sure you have received all the information on the Council Tax due for that property. The Council Tax invoice will be posted to your address and it is to be paid by those who have signed the lease. Budget about £75+ per person per month depending on your area.

- **Heating/electricity** Be sure to find out how the flat is heated. Electric heating is expensive and is therefore not ideal. Some flats and houses have gas central heating though. Beware of renting a flat that shares a heating system with other flats as you lose some usage and cost control of the heating. Gas and electricity could be around £75 per month as a general budget figure.

- **Water** Water utility charges vary from area to area, but you need to allow around £20 per month. Water provision is not privatized in Scotland, so its costs are included in the Council Tax.

- **TV licence** The UK law requires all those who own a TV to pay for a TV licence. Fines for non-payment are punitive. Contact www.tvlicensing. co.uk/ to organize payment.

- **Telephone** Many people prefer to use a mobile phone rather than get a landline for their flat. This is a great idea if you are sharing your accommodation as it saves arguments over the phone bills. If you want a landline you will need British Telecom (BT) to install it (at an additional cost) and it will then cost you around £12 per month standing charge plus calls. Visit www.bt.com

DECIDING WHERE TO LIVE

Research is the best way of finding somewhere suitable to live. You need to consider your own circumstances in order to find a location that will be suitable, either in the short or longer term. You need to consider things like:

- where you are most likely to find work or be located for work;

- the type of schools/colleges, etc. required for your children;

- accessibility to travel to work, e.g. public transport;

- social considerations about the neighbourhood;

- local amenities.

Once you are clear about your own needs, then research using the internet, scan national and local UK newspapers, and watch regional UK TV news programmes (usually accessed through satellite TV channels) to give you a flavour of different UK areas.

For easy-access maps of the whole UK, visit www.streetmap.co.uk To find out about a local area, start with the local tourist information centre. For England visit www.visitengland.com/, for Scotland visit: www.visitscotland.com/ and for Wales visit: www.visitwales.com/ Also visit www.rightmove.co.uk/home.rsp which can provide a list of local rental and buying agents anywhere in the UK; at the same time you can search the accommodation that they have currently available.

RENTING

Not sure where to be based or if you like where you are planning to be based? Renting is probably your best option. Rental costs vary across the UK, but there tends to be more rental accommodation in London than elsewhere. Typically the sort of prices you can expect to pay in London are:

Average flat-share rental per month		Average one-bedroom flat rental per month	
East London	£400	East London	£600
West London	£500	West London	£700
South London	£400	South London	£600
North London	£500	North London	£700

For the rest of the UK, city rentals will be more expensive than more outlying areas, but you'll get more for your money. In urban areas there tends to be less property to rent, as most people buy. However, it is always worth shopping around to see what you can get for the money you want to spend.

Most accommodation in the UK is furnished, which usually includes living room, bedroom and kitchen furniture and items (usually including fridge, oven, washing machine or even a dishwasher!).

Properties tend to come in studio, one-bed, two-bed or three-bed flats. Detached or semi-detached houses (which are usually hard to find in

London) are popular in other areas of the country as they offer space and more privacy than flats.

Signing up and costs

When you've found a place you want to rent, you will be asked for several references and perhaps even interviewed before you will be accepted as a suitable tenant for your chosen property.

The rental agents or landlord will take a full inventory of the items at the property and a copy of the tenancy contract will be given to you. In most cases it is worth having it checked by a solicitor just to make sure you are getting what you agreed to! Once you are happy, you sign the contract, and your tenancy begins from the agreed date.

You will be expected to pay the first month's rent in advance and usually about six weeks' rent as a deposit. Some rental agencies will also charge you a fee for signing up, so check with each agent before you sign anything.

Other relevant contacts

www.gumtree.co.uk
www.letdirect.com
Flatfinder 020 7243 5544
www.rightmove.co.uk

27

Healthcare

ABOUT THE NATIONAL HEALTH SERVICE

The National Health Service (NHS) was set up in 1948 and is now the largest organization in Europe. It is recognized as one of the best health services in the world by the World Health Organisation.

Department of Health

This is the department that supports the government in improving the health and wellbeing of the population. The Department of Health started a programme of change in 2005, designed to make sure it provides leadership to the NHS and social care.

Making changes to the NHS

The Shifting the Balance of Power programme has been introduced by the government and aims to design a service centred around patients, putting them first. It aims to be faster, more convenient and offer more choice.

The main feature of the change has been to give locally-based groups called Primary Care Trusts (PCTs) the role of running the NHS and improving health in their areas. This has also led to new Strategic Health Authorities being created which cover larger areas and now take a more strategic role.

In Scotland, the NHS is divided into NHS Boards. The role of these Health Boards is the protection and improvement of the health of their respective residents through implementation of The Health Improvement Programme. This is intended to improve co-operation not only between Trusts but also with Local Authorities. Primary Care Trusts and Acute Hospital Trusts, responsible for acute hospital services, operate within the geographical boundaries of individual Health Boards.

NHS services

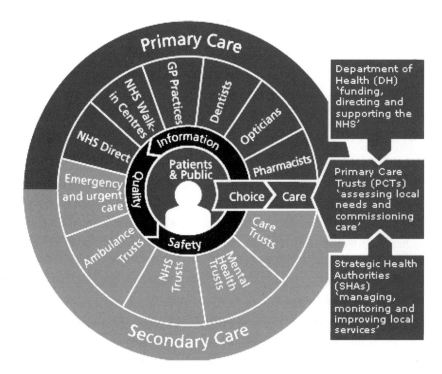

Primary care is the first point of contact most people have with the NHS and is delivered by a wide range of professionals, including family GPs (general practitioners or doctors), nurses, dentists, pharmacists and opticians.

This care focuses on the treatment of routine injuries and illnesses as well as preventive care, such as services to help people stop smoking. Primary care is mostly concerned with a patient's general health needs, but increasingly more specialist treatments and services are now becoming available in primary care settings closer to where people live.

About NHS Direct Online and the NHS Direct Telephone Service

The NHS's Direct Online health information enquiry service is intended for use if you cannot find the health information you need on the NHS Direct Online website at www.nhsdirect.nhs.uk The service aims to respond to all enquiries within five working days from receipt of your enquiry, but if your enquiry is more urgent the NHS offers a telephone service called NHS Direct on 0845 4647.

The information you submit to NHS Direct Online will be treated in the strictest confidence. Your enquiry will be researched by a skilled Health Information Professional, who will provide you with an individual response. The information you supply and the response provided will be stored securely by NHS Direct Online for at least five years.

NHS Direct Online's health information enquiry service provides information only about named health conditions. The service doesn't provide diagnoses, advice or counselling and is available only to residents in England. If you begin to feel ill, call NHS Direct immediately on 0845 4647 to get a nurse's advice.

NHS Walk-in Centres

NHS Walk-in Centres offer fast and convenient access to a range of NHS services, including health information, advice and treatment for a range of minor illnesses (coughs, colds, infections) and minor injuries (strains, sprains, cuts).

Most centres are open from early morning to late evening, seven days a week. The centres are run by experienced NHS nurses, and you don't need to make an appointment. Some newly-opened centres may offer different opening hours during the first few months.

Walk-in Centres are helping to improve the way in which thousands of patients get immediate treatment for troublesome minor health problems or injuries. To find your nearest centre visit, www.nhs.uk/England/No AppointmentNeeded/WalkInCentres/.

Emergency Services

Emergency Services in the UK are accessed by calling one telephone number: **999**. The call is free from any phone and you will be asked whether you require the services of: Police, Fire or Ambulance.

REGISTERING WITH A DOCTOR

Doctors (commonly known as GPs – General Practitioners) assess patients, provide preventive advice, prescribe medication and refer patients to other specialists. They may also provide contraception advice, sexual health services, maternity care and vaccinations. All GPs have a contract to provide a 24-hour service. This may include a GP out-of-hours call-out service or out-of-hours drop-in clinics that enable patients to visit without an appointment. During normal daytime hours, most GPs work on an appointment-only basis.

You can register with a GP by looking up your local practice and providing it with your medical card details. If you do not have a medical card, you should fill in form GMS1, which should be available at the surgery. Once you have been accepted as a patient, your medical records will be transferred to the new surgery and you will be sent a new medical card. When you register with a new GP it is a good idea to ask for an information leaflet about the surgery and its services and policies.

There are a number of reasons why you may not be able to register with your chosen GP. For example, the practice may be full or you may live too far away. If this is the case, simply choose another GP in your local area. If you have difficulty registering with a GP, the local PCT will be able to help. You can get the number from the phone book: look under 'Health Services' in the A–Z listing of local businesses and services. You can also get the number from NHS Direct on 0845 4647 or from the NHS websites (details of which are shown at the end of this chapter).

You can register with a GP on a permanent or temporary basis. If you are ill and staying in the area for three months or less, you can register with a GP as a temporary patient. If you are staying for longer than three months, you can register permanently with that GP if they are prepared to take you on.

FINDING A GP, DENTIST, OPTICIAN OR PHARMACY

The NHS websites (all shown below) allow you to search for your five nearest GPs, opticians, dentists and pharmacies. All you have to do is put in your postcode.

PRESCRIPTIONS

Prescriptions are issued by GPs and prescription charges apply to everyone except:

■ children under the age of 16;

■ young people under the age of 19 and in full-time education;

■ people over the age of 60;

■ people who suffer from a specific range of conditions.

Some other people may also be entitled to help with medical charges, such as those who qualify for the NHS Low Income Scheme. The NHS also provides a prescription pre-payment scheme, which enables patients who require repeat prescriptions to purchase prepaid certificates (PPCs).

All the information you require about prescriptions and GP services is available through the various NHS websites, details of which are shown below.

ALL THE CONTACTS YOU NEED

NHS telephone services

■ NHS Direct – 0845 46 47
A 24-hour nurse-led advice service for England, Wales and Northern Ireland.

■ NHS 24 – 08454 24 24 24
In Scotland, NHS 24 provides a health advice and support service.

■ NHS Direct Wales/Galw Iechyd Cymru – 0845 46 47 caters for Welsh speakers. There is also a separate website for NHS Direct Wales with information in English and Welsh.

NHS online services

www.nhs.uk/ The main gateway to all the NHS's services in the UK
www.nhsdirect.nhs.uk/ NHS for England

www.n-i.nhs.uk/ NHS in Northern Ireland
www.show.scot.nhs.uk/ NHS in Scotland
www.wales.nhs.uk/ NHS in Wales

The Isle of Man and the Channel Islands have separate independent health service structures. For more information please visit Isle of Man Government, States of Guernsey Government www.gov.im/dhss/health/ and States of Jersey Government www.health.gov.je/

Private health schemes

What's good about private medical cover? The main reason most people choose to 'go private' is that they want to avoid NHS waiting lists. They also want to choose their specialist, have more flexible visiting times, a private room and better-quality meals.

What's bad about private medical cover? It's very expensive, particularly if you want a good comprehensive policy, and premiums rise the older you get, although a few companies do not penalize you for getting older – so make sure you shop around.

Can you obtain private cover through your job? Some jobs already have private medical insurance as a free perk; others may offer it at a subsidised rate. This is well worth taking up and you may also be able to buy discounted cover for your partner and any children.

Do not expect cover for existing health problems Insurance is there for the unknown. This means any existing health condition will be excluded. Some existing conditions may become insurable after a waiting period set by the insurer, provided the condition does not recur during this period.

Which insurer to choose? Do not just pick a big-name insurer. There are smaller ones that offer very good service and cover. All insurance companies based in the UK and offering insurance are regulated, so you can buy with confidence.

Cash Plans A cash plan pays out a set amount if you need to go into hospital, and also for other healthcare needs such as glasses. Paid by regular subscription, cash plans have benefits and can top up your income, but they are not a substitute for insurance.

If you want to find private medical health cover, shop around on the internet. Sites such as www.thisismoney.co.uk/health and www.money supermarket.com all offer a facility for you to compare policies.

28

Transport

DRIVING IN THE UK

The road network in the UK is a mass of motorways, expressways and smaller roads. A total of 392,931 km of roads assist the population to get around with relative ease, although congestion does occur at peak times in the morning and evening. Around the many tourist hotspots the roads get jammed easily, so if you are planning to drive, allow extra time and check the travel reports. Live traffic updates are available 24 hours a day by calling 08700 660 115. Alternatively, the local radio and TV stations also carry travel bulletins throughout the day.

DRIVING LICENCES

If you already hold a driving licence you may be able to use it for up to 12 months before you will be required to take a UK driving test. Alternatively, you may be able to swap your existing licence for a British licence or apply for a provisional licence and then take a test.

The Driver and Vehicle Licensing Agency (DVLA) is the UK agency that manages all driving licence-related enquiries. Its website is www.dvla.gov.uk For international students needing advice on driving licences, a complete selection of Guidance Notes is available to download from www.ukcosa. org.uk/pages/guidenote.htm

RULES OF THE ROAD

- Drive on the left-hand side of the road.

- Give priority to traffic coming from the right.

- Pass (or overtake) on the outside (right) lane.

■ Do not pass on the inside (left) lane.

■ Do not block the middle lane if the inside lane is clear.

■ When approaching a roundabout, give priority to traffic approaching from the right, unless otherwise indicated.

■ At a junction there is no general priority rule, as priority is marked at most junctions. On a minor road you will see either a triangular 'GIVE WAY' or red 'STOP' sign. Many junctions will have only 'GIVE WAY' markings on the carriageway (dotted white lines and a white triangle on the carriageway). These signs must be obeyed.

■ All vehicles must give way to emergency services vehicles.

■ The use of a car horn is not permitted in built-up areas from 23.30 to 07.00 hours.

Drinking and driving

Alcohol can have a serious effect on judgement and your ability to drive. The legal limit is 80 mg of alcohol per 100 ml of blood, or 35 microgrammes of alcohol to 100 ml of breath. There are severe penalties for driving while under the influence of alcohol, and a big anti-drink and drive campaign operates in the UK.

Car accidents

If you are involved in an accident you must stop. Give details of your insurance to other drivers involved. If anyone is injured, you must also inform the police using the emergency number **999**.

Emergencies on motorways

Orange emergency telephones are situated at approximately half-a-mile intervals along motorways. They connect the caller to the Police Motorway Control Centre who can send the appropriate help, e.g. to breakdown recovery companies such as the AA (www.theaa.com), RAC (www.rac. co.uk), or the police, ambulance or fire brigade.

Special warning signals

Special warning signals are used on motorways to warn drivers of danger ahead. The panels are situated either on the central reservation or above each lane. On urban motorways, the signals are overhead, one for each lane.

Seatbelts

All new cars must have front and rear seatbelts fitted. A car which was not obliged to have seatbelts fitted at the time it was first used, does not need to have them fitted now. But if seatbelts are fitted they must be worn. For children under 14, it is the responsibility of the driver to ensure appropriate restraint is worn.

Mobile phones

It is an offence to use a mobile phone while driving. Offenders will be fined £30 initially, rising to a maximum of £1,000 if their case goes to court. Those caught breaking the ban will also get three penalty points on their licence for each offence. Under current laws, motorists can be prosecuted for using mobiles only if they fail to keep proper control of their vehicle.

Speed limits

Built-up areas: all vehicles, 30 mph (48 kph)

Single carriageway: 60 mph (96 kph) for cars, 50 mph (81 kph) for cars towing caravans or trailers, buses and coaches

Dual carriageways/motorways: 70 mph (112 kph) for cars, 60 mph (96 kph) for cars towing caravans or trailers.

Note: the maximum speed limits in Jersey and Guernsey are 40 mph (65 kph) and 35 mph (56 kph) respectively.

London congestion charge

The congestion charge is a £8 daily charge to drive in central London at certain times. Congestion charging was introduced on 17 February 2003 by the Mayor of London and is designed to reduce traffic congestion by encouraging people to use public transport. The money raised is being used to improve public transport in London.

The congestion charging zone operates across 8 square miles in the centre of London and has been expanded to the west of the City and West End. To check which roads are in the zone, view the Congestion Charge map located at www.cclondon.com/infosearch/dynamicPages/WF_ZoneCheck_W.aspx

The zone operates between 07.00 and 18.30, Monday to Friday. There is no charge at weekends or on public holidays.

Once you've paid the £8 London congestion charge you can enter and leave the zone as many times as you like during the day. The charge can be paid on a daily or weekly basis and you can also pay it up to 90 days before you arrive in London. All payments must be in UK currency.

You don't have to pay before you drive into the zone but you must pay before 22.00 that day to avoid penalty charges. The zone is monitored by cameras, which record all vehicle number plates and determine whether the charge has been paid. They recognize both British and European number plates.

The easiest way to pay is at www.cclondon.com or by phone on +44 (0) 20 7649 9122 – Minicom +44 (0) 20 7649 9123 using credit or debit cards. MasterCard and Visa cards are accepted – American Express and Diners Club aren't.

You'll need to provide your vehicle registration number, the date(s) you would like to pay the charge for, and your credit/debit card details. Keep a note of the receipt number as your proof of payment. You can also pay at special self-service machines in major car parks, at selected petrol stations and at shops displaying the congestion charge sign.

If you don't pay the charge the penalty charge/fine can be as much as £80. See Transport for London for full details: www.tfl.gov.uk/tfl/ or call +44 (0) 20 7649 9122.

Car hire

When arranging car hire, you are advised to book and pay before you leave. Prices for hiring a car vary from company to company and depend not only on the size and model of the car but the hire location as well (hiring a car at an airport is likely to be more expensive).

Motorcyclists

- On all journeys, the rider and pillion passenger on a motorcycle, scooter or moped must wear a protective helmet.

- Only one pillion passenger can be carried. He/she must sit astride the vehicle on a proper seat and should keep both feet on the footrests.

- Make yourself as visible as possible from the side as well as the front and rear by wearing fluorescent clothing or strips.

BUSES

Throughout the UK buses operate a variety of routes into towns, cities and some villages. The bus routes have depleted in recent years but it is still a convenient way to get around if you can find a bus timetable in your local area that suits your needs.

TRAVELLING BY COACH OR BUS

Most scheduled coach services are run by National Express and Scottish Citylink, allowing you to tour at your own pace on coaches which run to every major town and city in Britain. They are inevitably a little slower than trains but they are an economical alternative. Most coaches are very comfortable and many include refreshments on board. Details about local town and city buses can be obtained from local tourist information centres.

Brit Xplorer

This is a low-cost alternative for discovering the UK for overseas (non-British) passport holders. Brit Xplorer allows you an unlimited amount of journeys operated by National Express within a given period of time, depending on which Brit Xplorer pass you've opted for.

Travel tickets do not need to be booked. All you have to do is produce the Brit Xplorer to the driver at the time of departure. As long as the coach is not full, you can hop on board and travel. Visit www.nationalexpress.com/save/britxplorer.cfm

Mega Bus

For low-cost inter-city travel, also check www.megabus.com, which operate discounted bus services between London and 22 major cities across Britain.

London Buses

Every weekday over 6,800 scheduled buses carry around six million passengers on over 700 different routes in London, making it one of the largest and most comprehensive urban transport systems in the world.

In London there are two types of bus stop which are treated differently:

- White background with red roundel: Compulsory. Buses always stop here unless they are full.

- Red background with white roundel: Request. To stop a bus, put out your hand and the bus will stop, unless it is already full. To get off at a Request stop, ring the bell once and in good time to let the driver know. Night buses (prefixed with the letter N) treat all stops as Request stops.

Most of London's buses are red, but some come in other colours; all will display the London Bus Service sign.

London night buses

Nightbirds should note that there's a very good network of night buses (prefixed with the letter 'N') which get you around for a lot less than the price of a taxi. Nearly all of these start at or go via Trafalgar Square. Night buses run all night.

Bus fares

Bus fares can be paid to the driver/conductor once on board the bus. In London it isn't possible to buy a return ticket; therefore a separate ticket will need to be bought for each part of the journey (unless a Travelcard is purchased in advance). For maps of the London bus network, ask at Underground stations.

London tour buses

A good introduction to the sights of London is an open-top bus tour. Many companies offer hop-on, hop-off tours with full commentary in English, as well as digitally recorded audio versions in many other languages. Ask your local travel agent or tourist information office for further details.

BLACK CABS AND LICENSED MINICABS

London taxis, or 'black cabs' can be hailed in the street if they have a yellow 'For Hire' sign illuminated or located on designated ranks, which are situated at prominent places, including many mainline rail, Underground and bus stations. They are wheelchair-accessible and most have a variety of additional aids for disabled customers. The fares charged are regulated, and are clearly shown on a meter in the cab. And with safety paramount, all taxi vehicles and drivers must meet minimum standards (for drivers this includes passing the world-renowned 'Knowledge of London' examinations). Licensed vehicles are subject to regular checks by the Public Carriage Office.

Taxis outside London

Taxis outside London operate in much the same way: the vehicles and drivers are also licensed. Occasionally a traditional taxi can be found but they are more likely to be saloon cars. However, they will still have the illuminated 'For Hire' sign.

Private hire vehicles (minicabs)

The essential difference between taxis and private hire is that private hire journeys must be pre-booked through a licensed operator. Private hire vehicles cannot ply for hire in the street. So you can hire a minicab in person from minicab offices or by telephoning a local minicab office (telephone numbers can be found in the *Yellow Pages* telephone directory or at www.yell.co.uk). All minicab operators must hold an operating licence issued by the Public Carriage Office. Minicabs do not have a meter so it is advisable to agree a fare before starting your journey. It's unadvisable to accept an offer from drivers touting for business on the street; this is against the law.

LONDON UNDERGROUND

In 2009 London Underground carried over 1 billion passengers.

London Underground (or the 'Tube') runs for up to 20 hours a day (times vary according to location), every day and serves all parts of central London; it is one of the easiest ways to travel. Tickets can be purchased from ticket machines and ticket offices at all stations. Entering and leaving the Underground is made simple by the ticket-operated gates. At the end of your journey, if the value on your ticket is used up, the gate will open but your ticket will be retained. The Underground is divided into six fare zones, with Zone 1 covering central London. See the LU map to see what areas relate to which ticket zones. Copies of LU maps are available at LU stations and from www.tfl.gov.uk

NATIONAL RAIL

Britain's rail network connects over 2,000 stations with over 18,000 departures every day. Therefore, there is likely to be a train going your way! The network is modern and efficient and has state-of-the-art trains including the tilting Pendolino train which connects London with Birmingham, Liverpool, Manchester, Glasgow and Edinburgh.

The BritRail range of multi-journey passes and point-to-point tickets is specially designed to meet the needs of overseas visitors to Britain. These tickets can be used on all of the privatized train companies that operate mainline services in Britain and can be purchased from the shop at www.visitbritain.com or any railway station in the UK.

Index of Train Operating Companies (TOCs)

The following train operators operate in specific areas of the UK. You can contact each of the relevant train companies directly or use a centralized telephone and web service. The centralized service allows you to say where you are travelling from and then the relevant train times, train changes, ticket prices for your journey and train operators will be given to you. This service is offered at among others, http://www.nationalrail.co.uk/ National Rail telephone enquiry line: 0845 748 4950 and www.thetrainline.com/

Arriva Trains Wales www.arrivatrainswales.co.uk/

c2c www.c2c-online.co.uk/c2c_ticker_index.aspx

Central Trains www.centraltrains.co.uk/

Chiltern Railways www.chilternrailways.co.uk/

Eurostar www.eurostar.com

First Great Western www.firstgreatwestern.co.uk

First Great Western Link www.firstgreatwestern.co.uk

First ScotRail www.firstgroup.com/scotrail/

Gatwick Express www.gatwickexpress.com

Heathrow Connect www.heathrowconnect.com/

Heathrow Express www.heathrowexpress.com/

Hull Trains www.hulltrains.co.uk/

Island Line www.island-line.co.uk/

Merseyrail www.merseyrail.org/

Midland Mainline www.midlandmainline.com/Default.asp?version=7

National Express www.nationalexpress.com

Northern Rail www.northernrail.org/

one www.onerailway.com/

Silverlink www.silverlink-trains.com/

South Eastern Trains www.setrains.co.uk/setrains

South West Trains http://www.southwesttrains.co.uk/SWTrains

Southern www.southernrailway.com/

Thameslink www.thameslink.co.uk/

TransPennine Express www.tpexpress.co.uk/

Virgin Trains www.virgintrains.co.uk/

WAGN www.wagn.co.uk/

Wessex Trains www.wessextrains.co.uk/

GENERAL TIPS FOR TRAVELLING IN THE UK

■ Smoking is not permitted on the London Underground system or on buses, and is no longer allowed in any carriages on the national rail network.

■ Keep personal belongings with you at all times to avoid delays caused by security alerts (abandoned luggage may be destroyed).

■ Be aware that pickpockets and ticket touts operate in busy areas.

■ Travelling outside the 'rush hour' 08.00–09.30 and 17.00–18.00 Monday–Friday is easier, more comfortable and cheaper.

29

Moving to the UK

SHIPPING/AIR FREIGHT

Once you've decided on the key items you want to take, you'll need to consider how to get them moved to the UK. There are two main options: air or sea.

Shipping

Sea freight costs are worked out by volume so it is the cheapest method of delivery. However, it is also the slowest way to get your belongings to your new home. You should also be aware that Customs and Excise do make random checks which they charge you for – anything from about £25 upwards. All shipping companies should quote for everything except insurance, which you will need to get. You need to nominate the value of the goods and then pay either 3.5% of the value of the goods to cover loss only, or 5% for full insurance. With shipping and insurance you need to shop around. www.intlmovers.com/ is a one-stop shop to source an international moving company that suits your needs. Just enter where you are moving from and to, and up pops a list of companies that can quote for your move. For a list of all worldwide sea freight operators, go to http://products.kompass.com

Airfreight

Airfreight is a much quicker way of getting belongings to your new country but is considerably more expensive, with the costs being calculated on weight. Contact airlines and other airfreight specialists for quotes. The cost may be too prohibitive but is still worth considering. Post one request and get many offers for both sea and air freight moves from www.OneEntry.com For a list of all worldwide airfreight operators, go to http://products.kompass.com

Whichever route you choose, make sure you choose a company:

- that is well established and has a proven track record;

- is committed to overseas moving as its core business;

- that assumes door-to-door responsibility worldwide;

- that is big enough to cope but small enough to care;

- that has its own packers and is in the business for the long run.

DECIDING WHAT TO TAKE

How much do you really need? You may find that it will be cheaper to sell some items and buy them new in the UK once you arrive. There are usually lots of friends and family that will take items off your hands. Consider the costs of taking all your furniture and bulky items and ask yourself: Will they really all fit into my new home?

Most people find that moving house, as well as moving country, is a great time to have a good clear out of all those items in the loft, garage, shed, outhouse, etc. Remember, you are moving to a country where you can buy all the things you've ever needed and a whole lot more!

PETS IN THE UK

The Pet Travel Scheme (PETS) allows cats and dogs to enter the UK without the period of quarantine that was previously required.

To travel to the UK under the PETS scheme, the pet must:

- be fitted with a microchip;

- be vaccinated against rabies;

- be blood tested to show a satisfactory level of protection against rabies;

- be treated against ticks and a type of tapeworm;

- have a declaration of residency completed by the owner;

■ be issued with an official PETS certificate;

■ be issued with an Animal Welfare Export certificate.

The whole process will take a minimum of about seven months, as the blood test for the level of rabies protection must be taken at least six months prior to entry into the UK.

It is worth noting that certain breeds of dogs such as Pit Bull Terriers, Japanese Tosas, Dogo Argentinos and Fila Brasilieros, or any animal which appears to have been bred for fighting, will not be allowed entry.

For further information, visit www.defra.gov.uk/animalh/animindx.htm for an introduction to animal health and welfare from the UK Government and more details about the PETS scheme.

BEFORE YOU DEPART FOR THE UK

Here are just a few things we suggest you organize before your departure:

■ arrange appointments for relevant inoculations;

■ arrange travel/medical insurance;

■ notify doctor and obtain medical history/records, and details of medication where necessary;

■ obtain eye prescription from optician;

■ request dental records from dentist;

■ transfer to or set up new UK bank accounts;

■ cancel store cards;

■ notify credit card companies;

■ advise tax department you are leaving the county and get advice;

■ cancel service providers – electricity, gas, water, council tax, telecoms providers, TV licence, etc.;

- redirect mail through the Post Office;

- send out change of address cards;

- clear out unwanted belongings;

- put items you are not taking into storage;

- make a list of everything you are going to take;

- use up food from freezer;

- organize disconnection of domestic appliances;

- cancel any regular deliveries (milk, newspapers);

- take down curtains and blinds;

- pay all outstanding bills;

- make sure you have your driver's licence, car registration and insurance records;

- make arrangements for moving your pets and any house plants; they cannot usually be taken in the mover's van.

On the day

- pack small valuables separately;

- pack essential items in your hand luggage;

- confirm service meter readings and keep a spare copy of readings;

- switch off power and water supplies (if necessary);

- lock all windows and doors;

- deposit keys with estate or rental agent.

30

Arriving in the UK

You've finally arrived! If you've travelled by air, you will probably arrive at one of the main international airports in London – Heathrow or Gatwick, or one of the big regional airports – Manchester or Glasgow. If you have arrived by sea you will probably arrive at one of the Channel ports – Dover, Folkestone or Harwich are the most likely.

Once you've collected your baggage and passed through Customs, you will need to start your onward journey to your final destination and your new home. If you need to use trains, coaches or taxis, try to book them in advance so you can relax a little once you arrive. Likewise, if you are planning to stay a night before moving on, it would be best to book a hotel room in advance before you arrive in the UK.

LINKS FROM THE MAIN AIRPORTS

Heathrow Heathrow is one of the world's busiest airports. There are coach connections, a Tube station (on the Piccadilly line, marked in dark blue on the Tube map) and the 'Heathrow Express' train service to Paddington station in London.

Gatwick There are coach connections, and a train service from Gatwick to central London (Victoria or King's Cross stations, depending on which train you catch). There is also a 'Gatwick Express' train service direct to London's Victoria station.

Stansted There are local connections and coach services and a 'Stansted Express' train service to Liverpool Street station in London.

Luton There is a coach service and train service (via shuttle bus from the airport) to central London.

USING THE UNDERGROUND (TUBE)

All Tube stations feature on the famous London Underground map. This details the different Tube lines in different colours and allows you to see at which stations you can transfer from one line to another. If you are planning to use the Tube, remember that you may have to change trains to get to your destination. At some stations this can be difficult if you have a lot of luggage. The Tube can be extremely crowded at 'rush hour' on weekdays (Monday to Friday).

MONEY FOR YOUR IMMEDIATE NEEDS

When you arrive in the UK, you should have about £250 in cash and travellers' cheques for your immediate needs (meals, train fares, etc.). Avoid carrying any more cash in case it gets lost or stolen. Most shops and hotels will accept credit cards, and some will also accept payment by sterling travellers' cheques.

The vast majority of shops and services in the UK will accept payment in UK currency only. You may also be able to withdraw money from ATM ('cash') machines as long as you have a Personal Identification Number (PIN) for that card.

PUBLIC PHONE BOXES

In case your mobile phone isn't working, you will find public telephones at all airports, sea ports, railway stations, bus stations and on many streets. They accept coins from 20 pence upwards and most phone boxes accept credit/debit cards as well as coins. These can be purchased from most convenience shops and newsagents.

Useful contacts

Traveline

Web: www.traveline.org.uk Tel: +44 870 608 2 608 (from outside UK) 0870 608 2 608 (from inside UK) – lines usually open 8 a.m. to 8 p.m.

Information on transport services throughout the UK. The website includes a travel planner facility.

National Rail Enquiries
Web: www.nationalrail.co.uk Tel: 0044 20 7278 5240 (from outside UK) 08457 484950 (from within UK). Information on all UK rail services

Airport express train services
Heathrow Express: web: www.heathrowexpress.com Tel: 0845 600 1515
Gatwick Express: web: www.gatwickexpress.co.uk Tel: 0845 850 1530
Stansted Express web: www.stanstedexpress.co.uk Tel: 0845 8500 150

National Express coach services
Web: www.nationalexpress.com Tel: 08705 80 80 80

Scottish Citylink coach services
Web: www.citylink.co.uk Tel: 08705 50 50 50

Transport for London
Web: www.tfl.gov.uk Tel: 020 7222 1234 (24 hours). Covers bus, tube, train and other services in London.

The British Airport Authority
www.baa.co.uk Information about Heathrow, Gatwick, Stansted, Glasgow, Edinburgh, Aberdeen and Southampton airports.

31

Lifestyle and Leisure

The UK lifestyle, although heavily work-focused, still allows a 'community' atmosphere in most villages and towns and even in some cities. Most people are fairly relaxed but the British are a very proud people when it comes to national sports like football, rugby and cricket.

Depending on where you live or where you visit, you are never far from the sea. To give an idea of the UK's size, here are some facts and figures:

- With an area of about 242,000 sq km (93,000 sq miles), Britain is just under 1,000 km (about 600 miles) from the south coast to the extreme north of Scotland and just under 500 km (around 300 miles) across at the widest point.

- The coastline of Great Britain is 14,549 km (9,040 miles) with England and Wales, including islands, taking up 5,214 km (8,389 miles) of this figure and Scotland, including islands, 9,335 km (5,800 miles).

- The most northerly point on the British mainland is Dunnet Head, north-east Scotland, and the most southerly is Lizard Point, Cornwall.

- From areas of flat land, to 2,000 miles of navigable canals and several mountain ranges, the landscape is varied.

LEISURE ACTIVITIES

Pubs

You will find that pubs play a large part in British culture and are the most popular places to socialize are in and around city and town centres. In London, Leicester Square, Soho, Old Street and Charing Cross Road are probably the most central and popular areas for going out.

By law, you have to be over 18 years old to drink, buy or attempt to buy alcohol. It is also an offence for any person under the age of 18 to buy or attempt to buy alcoholic liquor or to consume alcohol on licensed premises. Although there are some exceptions. People aged 16 or 17 may consume wine, beer or cider on licensed premises (pubs/bars/restaurants) with a table meal. In England and Wales, an adult must order. In Scotland, no adult is required to be present.

The new licensing law has allowed many of Britain's 113,000 pubs, clubs and bars to apply for new longer opening licences, giving them flexible opening hours, with the potential to open 24 hours a day, seven days a week.

Cinemas and video/DVD hire

Cinemas are a good option on a cold or grey evening. The largest cinema in London is The Odeon (0870 5050 007 – www.odeon.co.uk) in Leicester Square, while The Empire, across the square, is another popular cinema. CineWorld is also one of the major cinema chains in the UK, as is Vue. Expect to pay around £6.50 for an adult ticket. All films receive a UK classification before they are released. They are: U=universal, suitable for anyone aged four or over; PG=parental guidance, suitable for general viewing but some scenes may not be suitable for children without guidance from parents; 12=no one under 12 admitted unless with an adult; 15=no one under 15 permitted; 18=no one under 18 permitted. Video and DVD hire shops are located across the UK. The classification of each film is shown on the cover.

Sport

The main sports the Brits are passionate about and/or take part in are: rugby, football, cricket, golf, tennis, Formula One and athletics. With London hosting the 2012 Olympics, it is hoped that many more people will take up a sport as a leisure pursuit.

Eating out

Whether it's a pub lunch or a gourmet dinner, there are lots of restaurants across the UK serving some of the best food in the world.

Theatre

London's West End is most famous for its large-scale productions. The Royal National Theatre and the Barbican Theatre host a wide variety of quality dramas. For dance, opera and music, the London Coliseum, Sadler's Wells and the Royal Opera House are at the forefront. Regional theatre across the UK also features top West End productions on tour and offer a really good evening out. Listings of shows are available in national and London newspapers and magazines such as *Time Out*. For discounted tickets for West End shows and for booking tickets on the day of the performance, either go direct to the theatre for standby tickets or returns (ring ahead for availability) or, for genuine discount tickets, buy in person from the **tkts** booth in the clocktower building on the south side of London's Leicester Square and at Canary Wharf Docklands Light Railway Station.

Useful websites

www.pubsulike.co.uk/
www.londontown.com/
www.londinium.com/
www.touchlondon.co.uk/
www.london-eating.co.uk/
www.fancyapint.com/
www.ugccinemas.co.uk
www.myvue.com/
www.gumtree.com/
www.londonolympics2012.com/
home.skysports.com/
www.rfu.com/
www.thefa.com/
www.icc-cricket.com/
www.toptable.co.uk/
www.londontheatre.co.uk/
www.officiallondontheatre.co.uk/tkts

WHERE TO GO AND WHAT TO DO

Wherever you are going to be based in the UK, famous historical and picturesque places are never far away.

From London to:	Driving Miles	Air	Train	Coach
Bath	106	n/a	1hr 30min	2hr 25min
Belfast	340	1hr 25min	10hr 35min	11hr
Birmingham	114	n/a	1hr 45min	2hr 40min
Brighton	51	n/a	51min	1hr 45min
Cambridge	56	n/a	50min	1hr 50min
Canterbury	62	n/a	1hr 35min	1hr 45min
Cardiff	145	n/a	2hr 05min	3hr 5min
Chester	179	n/a	2hr 40min	5hr 30min
Durham	255	n/a	3hr	6hr
Edinburgh	393	1hr 30min	4hr 30min	8hr 45min
Exeter	174	n/a	2hr 30min	4hr 15min
Glasgow	402	1hr 30min	5hr 30min	7hr 55min
Inverness	568	1hr 45min	8hr 10min	12hr 26min
Jersey	220	1hr	6hr 55min	7hr 55min
Liverpool	193	n/a	3hr	4hr 30min
Manchester	184	1hr	2hr 40min	4hr 15min
Newcastle-upon-Tyne	270	1hr 10min	3hr	6hr 25min
Norwich	115	n/a	1hr 50min	2hr 40min
Oxford	64	n/a	1hr 05min	1hr 30min
Portsmouth	70	n/a	1hr 40min	2hr 15min
Salisbury	84	n/a	1hr 30min	2hr 40min
Southampton	80	n/a	1hr 20min	2hr
Stratford-upon-Avon	121	n/a	2hr 12min	2hr 45min
Windermere	259	n/a	4hr 10min	6hr 55min
York	188	n/a	2hr	4hr 15min

NB: All times are approximate

TOP TOURIST ATTRACTIONS IN LONDON

1. Tate Modern, Sumner Street, SE1. Tel: (020) 7887 8000.
   www.tate.org.uk

2. The London Eye, Jubilee Gardens, SE1. Tel: (0870) 500 0600.
   www.londoneye.com

3. The Tower of London, Tower Hill, EC3. Tel: (020) 7709 0765.
   www.hrp.org.uk

4. National Gallery, Trafalgar Square, WC2N 5DN. Tel: +44 (0)20 7747
   2885. Email: information@ng-London-org.uk
   http://wwwnationalgallery.org.uk

5. Natural History Museum, Cromwell Road, SW7 5BD. Tel: +44 (020)
   7942 5000. Email: info@nhm.ac.uk
   http://www.nhm.ac.uk/exclusive-events

6. Madame Tussaud's Marylebone Road, NW1. Tel: (020) 7935 6861. http://www.madame-tussauds.com/
7. British Museum Great Russell Street, WC1. Tel: (020) 7636 1555. http://www.thebritishmuseum.ac.uk
8. Science Museum, Exhibition Road, SW7 2DD. Tel: +44 (0)20 7942 4000. Email: sciencemuseum@nmsi.ac.uk http://www.sciencemuseum.org.uk/about_us/doing_business_with_us/corporate_and_private_events.aspx
9. Victoria & Albert Museum, Cromwell Road, SW7 2RL. Tel: +44 (0)20 7942 2000. Email: vanda@vam.ac.uk http://www.vam.ac.uk/resources/corporate
10. National Maritime Museum, Romney Road, Greenwich SE10 9NF. Tel: +44 (0)20 8312 6585. Email: bookings@nmm.ac.uk http://www.nmm.ac.uk/business-and-hire

OTHER TOP LONDON ATTRACTIONS

▨ Buckingham Palace – home of the Queen.

▨ Leicester Square – the heart of the West End and Theatreland.

▨ St Paul's Cathedral – the famous cathedral designed by Sir Christopher Wren.

▨ Tower Bridge – one of London's best-known landmarks.

▨ London Planetarium – where you can look at the night sky.

▨ Oxford Street – Europe's longest shopping street.

▨ Piccadilly Circus – home of the famous Eros statue and giant illuminated billboards.

▨ Regent Street – famous shops include Hamley's toy store and the Liberty department store.

▨ Westminster Abbey – the venue for coronations.

OTHER TOP UK ATTRACTIONS

Alton Towers, Staffordshire www.altontowers.com/resort/

Legoland, Windsor www.lego.com/legoland/windsor/
Windsor Castle, Berkshire www.windsor.gov.uk/attractions/castle.htm
Edinburgh Castle, Edinburgh www.historic-scotland.gov.uk/
Chester Zoo, Cheshire www.chesterzoo.org/
The Eden Project, Cornwall www.edenproject.com/
Kew Gardens, London www.rbgkew.org.uk/welcome.html
Roman Baths and Pump Room, Bath www.romanbaths.co.uk/
Blackpool Pleasure Beach, Lancashire www.blackpoolpleasurebeach.com/
York Minster, Yorkshire www.yorkminster.org/

EUROSTAR AND EUROTUNNEL

With Europe so close, the Eurostar and Eurotunnel offer a quick and relaxing way to be in the centre of Paris in less than three hours.

- Eurostar – a direct link between Paris, Lille, Brussels and London (St Pancras), Ashford (Kent) on Eurostar trains. This service is for foot passengers only and runs every hour (between 05.00 and 20.00) and takes approximately 3 hours. Contact: 08705 186186.

- Eurotunnel – carries passengers and their vehicles and operates between Calais and Folkestone. Trains run 24 hours. Between 06.00 and midnight there are three trains an hour, between midnight and 06.00 a service operates every two hours. Contact: 08705 353535.

Need more ideas on things to do?
www.english-heritage.org.uk/
www.visitwales.com/
www.visitbritain.com/vb3-en-gb/default.aspx
www.nationaltrust.org.uk/main/
www.timeout.com/london/
www.hrp.org.uk/webcode/home.asp

32

Useful Information – Things You Need to Know

CURRENCY IN THE UK

The UK has a decimal-based currency known as sterling, or more commonly known as pounds. 100 pence equals £1 (one pound in sterling).

A variety of coinage and notes are available and are detailed below. The UK has not converted to the Euro coins and notes. However, when travelling to some of the other main European countries, e.g. France, Spain, Italy, Greece, you should be aware that they all use the single Euro currency.

UK coins

1 pence   = 1p (smallest coin, copper coloured)
2 pence   = 2p (copper coloured)
5 pence   = 5p (smallest silver coin)
10 pence = 10p (silver coin)
20 pence = 20p (silver coin)
50 pence = 50p (largest silver coin)
£1   = 100p (gold coloured)
£2   = 200p (largest gold coloured)

UK notes

£5   = 500p Blue/green colour
£10   = 1000p Brown colour
£20   = 2000p Purple colour
£50   = 5000p Red/orange colour

TIPPING

Tipping in the UK is not always appropriate. If you feel you received good service and you want to show your appreciation, here is a guide to customary practice.

- Hotels
  Most hotel bills include a service charge, usually 10–12%. Where a service charge is not included in a hotel restaurant, it is customary to give 10–15% of the restaurant bill and for rooms an optional amount to room staff.

- Restaurants
  Some restaurant bills include a service charge; where a service charge is not included, it is customary to leave a tip of 10–15% of the bill. Some restaurants now include a suggested tip in the bill total.

- Taxis
  10–15% of the fare.

- Porterage
  Discretionary.

- Hairdressers
  Discretionary

COST OF LIVING IN THE UK

London is one of the world's most expensive cities. The *Guardian* newspaper printed a report in July 2009 stating that London is 16th on the world list, albeit falling 13 places from 2008. Across the world, living in a capital city is more expensive than living in the provinces. In the UK, living in Manchester, for example, is 16% cheaper than London.

As with most comparisons, the 'Cost of Living in the UK' really does depend on each individual's situation. However, often a person staying in the UK for a few years can effectively minimize major expenses, by renting a car, sharing a house and using public transport wherever possible.

One thing you shouldn't do is keep converting the cost of an item from UK pounds into your previous currency. It can seriously distort your view and enjoyment of UK life!

The following are some rough examples of what it can cost to live in the UK:

UK COST OF ACCOMMODATION

Flat-share	Rental per month	One-bedroom flat	Rental per month
East London	£400	East London	£600
West London	£500	West London	£700
South London	£400	South London	£600
North London	£500	North London	£700

UK COST OF FOOD AND DRINK

Average weekly grocery bill	£60
Average pub meal	£6
Average restaurant meal	£18
Pint of beer	£2.50–£3
Average bottle of wine	£8
Average meal for two in mid-priced restaurant	£40

UK COST OF TRANSPORTATION

Weekly Zone 1–6 Travelcard	£30
Monthly Zone 1–2 Travelcard	£70
London to Edinburgh by train	£92
London to Cambridge/Brighton by train	£20
Mid-sized car rental for a weekend	£70
Return budget flight to Spain	£150
Eurostar return ticket to Paris	£110
Return flight to Ireland	£100

UK COST OF ENTERTAINMENT

Movie	£7–£10
West End play	£25

OPENING A BANK ACCOUNT

Ideally you should open a UK-based bank account at least five weeks before you leave for the UK. Your existing bank at home should be able to organize this for you through affiliations it has with UK banks. Then all you have to do is arrange to collect your cheque book and debit card from your new local branch when you arrive in the UK.

If you can't or haven't made arrangements before you leave, you can expect opening a UK bank account to take two weeks or more, and be a tedious process of form filling and identification. Most banks request you open a bank account in person. The type of items that they require you to show as proof of identity varies, but could include at least two of the following items:

■ passport;

■ national identity card;

■ residence permit;

■ national driving licence;

■ tenancy agreement for your new home in the UK;

■ a letter from your employer in the UK confirming your address, salary, etc.;

■ proof of your previous or permanent address in the country you came from;

■ a letter from your previous bank or your agreement that you new bank can contact it.

This list is not exhaustive. However, the best approach if you are going into a UK bank to open an account is to take as many original documents with you as possible. Banks will not accept copies, so remember to take the originals.

HIGH STREET BANKS AND BUILDING SOCIETIES

There are lots of well-known high street banks and building societies in the UK. The following is a list of some of the most common ones:

Alliance and Leicester
Barclays Bank

HBOS
HSBC
Lloyds TSB
Royal Bank of Scotlans
Natwest
Clydesdale Bank

Most banks and building societies require you to operate your bank account for a period until they will provide/offer you with additional services. This gives them a chance to see your salary being paid in and your bills being paid out. They will also check that you will be using your debit card for cash withdrawals and payments responsibly. Depending on which bank you open your account with, there will be a different time period before you can ask for an overdraft facility, a more complex bank account or a credit card.

Building societies

These are different from banks. Building societies are traditionally known more for savings accounts and mortgage lending. However, in recent years a number have been bought out by banks and have also diversified their services to include current accounts, cash machines, credit cards, foreign exchange desks, insurance and loans.

Online banks

All the major UK banks offer internet banking services, so you can manage your account remotely.

However, there are also a number of banks that operate just an online service and consequently do not have a high street presence. They are usually subsidiaries of the leading financial banking providers listed above but operate as separate businesses. Opening an account with one of these internet banks still requires proof of identity, but proof (originals only) has to be sent by post. You will then have to wait until checks have been conducted before your account is open and fully functional. Documents will then be returned to you by post.

Further information
The British Bankers' Association represents all the UK's financial services firms and also provides help on how to open a bank account. It can be contacted at www.bba.org.uk

POSTAGE SYSTEM

Sending mail within Britain
Royal Mail is the official mail service in Britain. It provides two main services:

- first class aims to deliver all First Class letters and packages by the next working day;

- second class aims to deliver all Second Class letters and packages within three working days.

The Royal Mail also offers 'Special Delivery' and 'Recorded' services, as well as international airmail services to all locations across the world.

There are also a number of private courier services, listed in the *Yellow Pages* and at www.yell.co.uk, which you can use for UK or international deliveries.

For further information about sending mail within Britain, phone Royal Mail Customer Services on +44 (0)8457 740 740 or visit www.royalmail.com

Sending mail from Britain
There are two options for sending mail weighing up to 2kg abroad: airmail and surface mail. Airmail is simple and quick, whereas surface mail is cheaper but takes longer.

All postal packets (excluding letters) to destinations outside the European Union are liable to examination by Customs authorities. It is important you check whether you need to fill in a Customs declaration before you post your package.

A detailed price list for airmail and surface mail is available from Post Offices or via the Royal Mail/Post Office website at www.royalmail.com

Postage stamps

Postage stamps may be bought from a variety of outlets, including newsagents, post offices, petrol stations and card shops. They are sold in books of six or 12 first- or second-class stamps.

Post office opening hours

Post offices are generally open 09.00–17.30, Monday to Friday. Main post offices are also open 09.00–12.30 on Saturday. Note that exact opening hours vary depending on the size and location of the branch. For information on individual post offices' opening times, call Post Office Enquiries on +44 (0)8457 223344.

VOTING

Who can vote?

To vote in parliamentary elections in the UK you must be a British citizen, a citizen of another Commonwealth country or of the Irish Republic, as well as being resident in the UK, aged 18 or over, included in the register of electors for the constituency and not subject to any legal incapacity to vote. Visit www.electoralcommission.org.uk for full details.

People not entitled to vote include members of the House of Lords, foreign nationals resident in the UK (other than Commonwealth citizens or citizens of the Irish Republic), some patients detained under mental health legislation, sentenced prisoners and people convicted within the previous five years of corrupt or illegal election practices.

To vote in your own country

Most countries will allow you to vote in elections back in your own country, provided you intend to return home at some point. Typically postal voting is the easiest to do, although your country's embassy may also have voting booths in its buildings located in the UK. To vote in your own country, you need to check you are on the electoral roll. If you aren't, you will need to speak to your embassy. Your country's government websites will carry details of voting procedures while you are abroad. Some of the main country sites are listed below:

www.elections.org.nz (New Zealand)
www.aec.gov.au (Australia)
www.elections.org.sa (South Africa)
www.elections.ca (Canada)

MEDIA

Every aspect of business and all sectors of industry and the services are represented and reported in the national press and media, including print, television, radio and online content. Printed media is by far the biggest source of information. The main national broadsheet newspaper for UK business audiences is *The Financial Times* (FT). This covers finance and investment, stock exchanges and commodity markets, employment and recruitment, mergers and acquisitions, market analysis and comment, industry sectors, marketing, personnel and international developments. Through FT.com there is also substantial online information, including a global archive of reports and news items covering the international business spectrum.

Other national broadsheets provide daily business news coverage, and each industry sector and sub-sector has at least one trade publication providing detailed coverage of specialized service and manufacturing industries in the UK. Nationwide media directories such as Pimms and Benns provide details of what is available in each trade sector. Printed and online information about local and regional markets is also available through Chambers of Commerce. Central government departments, such as the Department of Trade and Industry, and local government authorities provide regularly updated literature and online information for the business community. The BBC online service provides market and business information which is updated throughout each day.

UK media facts and figures

▪ Over 87% of UK households already have access to digital television. (Source: Ofcom end of March 2004.)

▪ Over 90% of the UK population listen to the radio, of which 12.7% listen to digital radio, also called DAB (Digital Audio Broadcasting).

This all adds up to lots of choice.

Useful sites

www.bbc.co.uk – 24hr news from the BBC with links to all the BBC's local radio stations across the UK

www.ft.com – *The Financial Times* online

www.ftse.com – in-depth information from the world-renowned index calculation specialist

www.insider.co.uk – Scotland's national business magazine. News, information and features for regional markets

www.economist.com – the UK's premier online and offline source for economics and business news and analysis

www.sky.com – latest satellite news from around the world and much more

www.newspapersoc.org.uk – details most newspaper titles in Britain

www.radio-now.co.uk – links to websites of all radio stations throughout Britain

www.itc.org.uk – details of all television stations throughout the UK

www.mediauk.com – directory of television, radio stations, and newspapers throughout the UK

INTERNET AND TELEPHONES

Internet cafes are everywhere in the UK and you can get hooked up for as little as 50p for half an hour.

If you can get connected at home, some of the major internet providers such as AOL are always running free trials for up to two months before you choose whether to sign up with them. With such competition in the market from Virgin, TalkTalk, Tiscali, Freeserve, AOL, BT, Wanadoo, etc., the monthly cost of connection continues to reduce. Even broadband service charges per month have significantly reduced in the past year. You can now get connected for free for a set period with most providers. It costs around £15 per month thereafter. Other costs for set-up and line rental are also applicable. (Source: www.moneysupermarket.com)

Landlines

British Telecom (BT) is the main telephone provider of landlines. BT will connect you within a day and charge you a quarterly standing charge for the connection.

Mobiles

Thanks to healthy competition, it is usually a lot cheaper to use a mobile telephone than to have a landline connected. Shop around, as most providers offer free talk minutes and texting bundles if you sign up for a 12-month contract.

Pay-as-you-go mobiles

The beauty of pay-as-you-go is you don't incur line rental or surcharges – you pay just for the time you use the phone. Pre-pay using top-up cards available from shops, newsagents, petrol stations and supermarkets and follow the instructions on the top-up card to register your phone credit. You will need to pay for a handset which could be £100 plus, or you may be able to use your original mobile phone and just buy a UK pre-pay SIM card for £10 to put into it.

Payphones

Located on streets and in airports, railway stations and other major public venues, public payphones will accept cash and credit card payments.

Using cash, the minimum fee for making a domestic call is 40p (includes 10p connection charge). Local and national calls are charged at 30p for the first 15 minutes, then 10p for each 7 minutes and 30 seconds thereafter.

Using credit or debit cards the minimum fee for local and national calls is 95p (includes 75p connection charge).

The minimum fee for international calls, calls to premium rate numbers, calls to mobile phones or calls made via the operator is £1.20 (includes a £1 connection charge).

VOLTAGE

The standard electrical voltage in Britain is 240 V AC, 50HZ. A three square-pronged adapter plug and/or electric converter for appliances is required.

PETS

Strict laws apply in the UK which require owners to care for their animals and make sure they do not suffer unnecessarily. The RSPCA employs many inspectors to prosecute owners and also care for abandoned animals.

All dogs in public places must wear a collar, showing the name and address of the owner, and must be kept under control. Dog owners should ensure their dogs do not foul footpaths.

REFUSE COLLECTION

Every home in Britain has a regular waste collection service. It is provided by the local council and will almost always be made on the same day, or days, each week. Contact your local council for details of which day(s) applies to your local address. To find your local council services, go to www.direct.gov.uk, look in your local telephone directory or look on www.yell.com

LANGUAGE

English is the official language in the UK, although regional English dialects exist and the traditional languages of Gaelic and Welsh are still spoken in some areas. If English is not your first language, it can be tiring listening and interpreting conversations every day, and even if you are a fluent English speaker it is possible that some regional accents will make it harder for you to understand what is being said. In certain areas of the UK you may find people speak quickly and you may feel embarrassed to ask them to repeat what they have said. However, in most cases, people will slow down or speak more clearly if you ask.

RELIGION

■ Christianity is the main religion in Great Britain. There were 41 million Christians in 2001, making up almost three-quarters of the population (72%). This group included the Church of England, Church of Scotland, Church in Wales, Catholic, and all other Christian denominations.

■ People with no religion formed the second-largest group, comprising 15% of the population.

■ About one in 20 (5%) of the population belonged to a non-Christian religious denomination.

■ Muslims were the largest religious group after Christians. There were 1.6 million Muslims living in Britain in 2001. This group comprised 3% of the total population and over half (52%) of the non-Christian religious population.

■ Hindus were the second-largest non-Christian religious group. There were over half a million Hindus (558,000), comprising 1% of the total population and 18% of the non-Christian religious population.

■ There were just over a third of a million Sikhs (336,000), making up 0.6% of the total population and 11% of the non-Christian religious population.

■ There were just over a quarter of a million Jewish people (267,000), constituting 0.5% of the total population and 9% of the non-Christian religious group.

■ Buddhists numbered 149,000 people in 2001, comprising 0.3% of the population of Great Britain.

Geographical religious breakdown

Based on the UK Government's 2001 population census:

■ people from non-Christian religions are more likely to live in England than in Scotland or Wales. In 2001 they made up 6% of the population in England, compared with only 2% in Wales and 1% in Scotland;

■ people from Jewish, Hindu, Buddhist, Muslim and Sikh backgrounds were concentrated in London and other large urban areas. Christians and those with no religion were more evenly dispersed across the country.

UTILITIES

There are an increasing number of companies offering utility services such as gas and electricity. Some of the more popular or useful sites and contact details are listed below:

Gas and electricity

www.uswitch.com – compare gas and electricity prices and switch suppliers
www.house.co.uk – British Gas
www.theenergypeople.com – services from Scottish Power

Water and sewerage

www.ofwat.gov.uk/aptrix/ofwat/publish.nsf/Content/watercompanyaddresstelephone – the UK regulator provides a full list of all the UK water and sewerage companies with their contact details

Council tax

www.direct.gov.uk – provides the latest information on UK public services
www.voa.gov.uk/ – details the council tax bands for all UK properties

TIME

Every year at the end of March, the UK changes to British Summer Time and the clocks go forward one hour. Towards the end of October, the clocks are put back by one hour and time reverts to Greenwich Mean Time (GMT).

BANK HOLIDAY DATES

The expected dates of bank and public holidays in England, Wales and Scotland for 2010 and 2011 are listed below.

When the usual date of a bank or public holiday falls on a Saturday or Sunday, a 'substitute day' is given, normally the following Monday. For example, in 2009 Boxing Day was on Saturday 26 December, so there was a substitute bank holiday on Monday 28 December.

England and Wales

There are currently eight permanent bank holidays in England and Wales.

England and Wales	2010	2011
New Year's Day	1 January	3 January*
Good Friday	2 April	22 April
Easter Monday	5 April	25 April
Early May Bank Holiday	3 May	2 May
Spring Bank Holiday	31 May	30 May
Summer Bank Holiday	30 August	29 August
Christmas Day	27 December*	26 December*
Boxing Day	28 December*	27 December*

*substitute day

Scotland

There are nine statutory bank holidays across the whole of Scotland. There are also other public or local holidays which can be determined by local authorities, based on local tradition. Since 2007, St Andrew's Day has been an alternative,voluntary public holiday, which can replace an existing local holiday.

Businesses and schools are not necessarily closed on Scottish bank holidays, and the Scottish banks follow the English and Welsh bank holidays for business reasons.

Scotland	2010	2011
New Year's Day	1 January	3 January*
2nd January	4 January*	4 January*
Good Friday	2 April	22 April
Early May Bank Holiday	3 May	2 May
Spring Bank Holiday	31 May	30 May
Summer Bank Holiday	2 August	1 August
St Andrew's Day	30 November	30 November
Christmas Day	27 December*	26 December*
Boxing Day	28 December*	27 December*

*substitute day

UK national saint days

1 March	St David's Day, national day of Wales.
17 March	St Patrick's Day, national day of Northern Ireland and the Republic of Ireland.
23 April	St George's Day, national day of England.
30 November	St Andrew's Day, national day of Scotland.

WEATHER AND CLIMATE

Whatever the season, the British weather is liable to change from day to day, so if you're wondering what to pack, a good idea is to take layers, a waterproof coat or jacket and an umbrella.

Autumn (September–November)

In Autumn there can be very warm days, but equally there can be very cold ones too! Temperatures fluctuate around the 7 to 14 degrees Centigrade mark but are likely to be much warmer in September than November.

Winter (December–early March)

Winter sees Britain's shortest and coldest days (about 7–8 hours of daylight) but these can be crisp and bright. Temperatures fluctuate from around 1 to 5 degrees Centigrade.

Spring (March–May)

In Spring you might enjoy wonderful sunny weather, but then it might also be cold and wet. Temperatures fluctuate from around 6 to 11 degrees Centigrade. May has warm days – up to about 18 degrees Centigrade.

Summer (June–August)

Most days in summer are warm, but evenings can be cool. Temperatures average around 14–20 degrees Centigrade, although they reach 28 degrees Centigrade and above on some days.

There is quite a difference in temperature between Scotland and southern England. Generally, the further north, the colder it is likely to be.

Europe's climate is as variable as everything else about the Continent. In northwestern Europe – Benelux, Denmark, southwestern Norway, most of France and parts of Germany, as well as the British Isles – the climate is basically a cool temperate one, with the chance of rain all year round and no great extremes of either cold or hot weather.

There is no bad time to travel in most of this part of the Continent, although the winter months between November and March can be damp and miserable – especially in the upland regions – and obviously the summer period between May and September sees the most reliable and driest weather.

AVERAGE TEMPERATUES IN EUROPE

	Jan	Feb	March	April	May	June	July	Aug	Sept	Oct	Nov	Dec
Amsterdam	4/40	5/42	9/49	13/56	18/64	21/70	22/72	22/71	19/67	14/57	9/48	6/42
Brussels	4/40	7/42	10/51	14/58	18/65	22/72	23/73	22/72	21/69	15/60	9/48	6/42
Dublin	8/46	8/47	10/50	13/55	15/60	18/65	20/67	19/67	17/63	14/57	10/51	8/47
Lisbon	14/57	15/59	17/63	20/67	21/71	25/77	27/81	28/82	26/79	22/72	17/63	15/58
London	6/43	7/44	10/50	13/56	17/62	20/69	22/71	22/71	19/65	14/58	10/50	7/45
Madrid	9/47	11/52	15/59	18/65	21/70	27/80	31/87	30/85	25/77	19/65	13/55	9/48
Paris	6/43	7/45	12/54	16/60	20/68	23/73	25/76	24/75	21/70	16/60	10/50	7/44
Rome	11/52	13/55	15/59	19/66	23/74	28/82	30/87	30/86	26/79	22/71	16/61	13/55

Temperatures are quoted in Centigrade and Fahrenheit

WHAT TO WEAR IN THE UK

If you come from a warm climate, you may find it uncomfortable to wear heavy winter clothing. Not everyone will find the British style of dress different but, for some, it may seem immodest, unattractive, comical or simply drab.

FITNESS

It is part of every day culture in the UK to go to the gym or take some form of exercise. However, very few tend to stick with their good intentions. A number of major employers across the UK have gyms and other sports facilities on-site to encourage their employees to have a healthy mind and body.

There are a number of major health club chains in the UK. This is just a selection. Check to see what special introductory offers they may have running.

www.lafitness.co.uk
www.davidlloydleisure.co.uk
www.virginactive.co.uk
www.cannons.co.uk

33

Crossing the Cultural Divide

The UK is a diverse and multi-ethnic society, where people of all backgrounds are welcome and their involvement in local communities is valued.

The UK is made up of three different countries and a province: England, Scotland, Wales and the province of Northern Ireland. These countries all have very different characters and identities.

The UK has a long tradition of welcoming migrants and refugees from around the world, many of whom have settled here permanently.

All major world religions are represented – mosques, Sikh temples, synagogues and Buddhist and Hindu places of worship can be seen alongside a whole range of Christian churches, from Anglican and Roman Catholic through to Nonconformist and Orthodox.

Many languages are represented as well. The most widely-spoken South Asian language in the UK is Punjabi, followed by Urdu, Bengali and Gujarati. The main Chinese dialects spoken in the UK are Cantonese and Mandarin.

All this diversity means that, when you come to the UK, you will find it easy to settle in. You will also develop an enhanced understanding of different cultures by meeting others from an enormous variety of religious and national backgrounds.

WHAT IS CULTURE SHOCK?

'Culture shock' describes the impact of moving from a familiar culture to one which is unfamiliar. It is an experience described by people who have travelled abroad to work, live or study. It can affect anyone and includes the shock of a new environment, meeting lots of new people and learning the ways of a different country. It also includes the shock of being separated from the important people in your life. Our emotions when moving to a new country go on a real rollercoaster ride! The following factors contribute to culture shock:

Food

You may find British food strange. It may taste different, or be cooked differently, or it may seem bland or heavy. Try to find a supplier of familiar food, and eat plenty of fresh fruit and vegetables.

Social roles

Social behaviours may confuse, surprise or offend you. For example, you may find people appear cold and distant or always in a hurry. This is particularly likely in the centres of large cities.

'Rules' of behaviour

As well as the obvious things that hit you immediately when you arrive, such as sights, sounds, smells and tastes, every culture has unspoken rules which affect the way people treat each other. The British generally have a reputation for punctuality. In business and academic life, keeping to time is important. Arranging to meet to see a film at 8 p.m. means arriving at 8 p.m. But if you are invited to visit someone's home for dinner at 8 p.m., you should probably aim to arrive at about ten minutes after eight. These subtle differences can be difficult to grasp and can contribute to culture shock.

Values

You may come to notice that people from other cultures may have very different views of the world from yours. Cultures are built on deeply-embedded sets of values, norms, assumptions and beliefs. As far as possible, try to suspend judgement until you understand how parts of a culture fit together into a coherent whole.

A MODEL OF CULTURE SHOCK

The process of culture shock can be illustrated by a model known as the 'W' curve (see diagram). This model may not relate to your experience or only partially. Sometimes the process is faster or slower. Many people go through different phases of the process, so parts of the curve in the diagram may repeat themselves. The process can be broken down into five stages:

Adapted from 'Orientated for Success', edited by M Marker, Australian International Development Assistance Bureau, 1990.

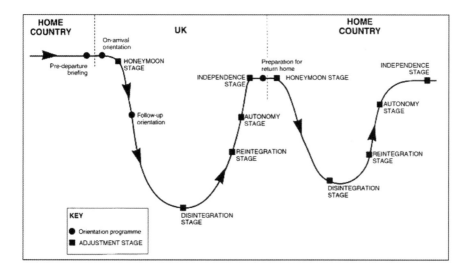

1. The 'honeymoon' stage

When you first arrive in a new culture, differences are intriguing and you may feel excited, stimulated and curious. At this stage you are still protected by the close memory of your home culture.

2. The 'disintegration' stage

A little later, differences create an impact and you may feel confused, isolated or inadequate as cultural differences intrude and familiar supports (e.g. family or friends) are not immediately available.

3. The 're-integration' stage

Next you may reject the differences you encounter. You may feel angry or frustrated, or hostile to the new culture. At this stage you may be conscious mainly of how much you dislike it compared with home. Don't worry, as this is quite a healthy reaction. You are reconnecting with what you value about yourself and your own culture.

4. The 'autonomy' stage

Differences and similarities are accepted. You may feel relaxed, confident, more like an old hand as you become more familiar with situations and feel well able to cope with new situations based on your growing experience.

5. The 'independence' stage

Differences and similarities are valued and important. You may feel full of potential and able to trust yourself in all kinds of situations. Most situations become enjoyable and you are able to make choices according to your preferences and values.

EFFECTS OF CULTURE SHOCK

- You may find your health is affected and you may get headaches or stomach aches.

- You may find it difficult to concentrate.

- You may become more irritable or tearful.

How to help yourself

- Simply understand that this is a normal experience which may in itself be helpful.

- Keep in touch with home by telephone, letter or email.

- Don't go home too often as this will make settling more difficult.

- Have familiar things around you that have personal meaning, such as photographs or ornaments.

- Find a supplier of familiar food.

- Eat a healthy and balanced diet.

- Take regular exercise.

- Make friends with people in a similar position, as they will understand what you're feeling.

- Find someone to talk to who will listen uncritically and with understanding, rather than isolating yourself.

- Students should make use of the services offered by their college including counselling, group activities and social events.

Culture shock is entirely normal, usually unavoidable and not a sign that you have made a mistake or that you won't manage. In fact, there are very positive aspects of culture shock. The experience can be a significant learning experience, making you more aware of aspects of your own culture as well as the new culture you have entered.

34

Useful Contacts

100 Operator (for help with calls locally, nationally and to the Republic of Ireland)

155 International Operator (for help with international calls or calls to a ship)

118 500 Directory Enquiries (can supply phone numbers for individuals and businesses in Britain if given name and location)

118 505 International Directory Enquiries (as above but for overseas individuals/businesses)

999 Emergency Services (police, fire, ambulance)

Some special phone codes worth knowing include:
Toll-free: **0500/0800**
Local call rate applies: **0845**
National call rate applies: **0870**

UK EMBASSIES AND HIGH COMMISSIONS

Each country has an overseas representative based in the UK. Here are some of the most popular:

New Zealand High Commission. Tel: (020) 7930 8422.
http://www.nzembassy.com/
Bangladeshi High Commission. Tel: (020) 7584 0081.
http://www.bangladeshhighcommission.org.uk/
Brazilian Embassy. Tel: (020) 7499 0877. http://www.brazil.org.uk/
South African Embassy. Tel: (020) 7451 7299.
http://www.southafricahouse. com/
American Embassy. Tel: (020) 7499 9000. http://www.usembassy.org.uk/

Canadian High Commission. Tel: (020) 7258 6600 General Enquiries
   http://www.dfait-maeci.gc.ca/canadaeuropa/united_kingdom/
Japanese Embassy. Tel: (020) 7465 6500. http://www.uk.emb-japan.go.jp/
Thai Embassy Tel: (020) 7589 2944. www.thaiinuk.com
Australian High Commission. Tel: (020) 7379 4334. www.australia.org.uk
Indian High Commission. Tel: (020) 7836 8484. http://www.hcilondon.net/
Embassy of Chile. Tel: (020) 7580 6392. E-mail embachile@embachile.co.uk
Embassy of China. Tel: (020) 7299 4049. http://www.chinese-embassy.org.uk
Indonesian Embassy. Tel: (020) 7499 7661. http://www.indonesianembassy.
   org.uk/
Embassy of Kenya. Tel: (020) 7636 2371/5
Malaysian Embassy. Tel: (020) 7235 8033
Embassy of Mexico. Tel: (020) 7499 8586. http://www.embamex.co.uk/
Embassy of North Korea. Tel: (020 8992 4965
Embassy of Nepal – Tel: (020) 7229 1594/6231. http://www.nepembassy.
   org.uk/
Embassy of Pakistan. Tel: (020) 7664 9200. http://www.pakmission-uk.
   gov.pk
South Korean Embassy. Tel: (020) 7227 5500/2. http://korea.embassyhome-
   page.com/
Embassy of Singapore. Tel: (020) 7235 8315. http://www.mfa.gov.sg/london/
Sri Lankan Embassy. Tel: (020) 7262 1841–7. http://www.slhclondon.org/
United Arab Emirates Embassy (UAE). Tel: (020) 7581 1281
Embassy of Venezuela. Tel: (020) 7584 4206/7. http://www.venezlon.co.uk/
Embassy of Vietnam. Tel: (020) 7937 1912

INDEPENDENT VISA ADVICE

www.amblercollins.com

GOVERNMENT DEPARTMENTS

www.ukvisas.gov.uk Government department site for UK visas
www.dfes.gov.uk/ Department for Children, Schools and Families
www.hmce.gov.uk HM Customs and Excise advice on importing goods into
   the UK.
www.ind.homeoffice.gov.uk The immigration and nationality section of the

Home Office is designed to help you understand the UK's immigration rules.

www.workpermits.gov.uk Work Permits (UK) administer work permit arrangements for the UK Government.

www.hmrc.gov.uk/ Features news and information relating to taxation and National Insurance in the UK.

www.dwp.gov.uk/lifeevent/benefits/ni_number.asp Provides information relating to how to obtain a National Insurance Number, and about pensions, benefits and services.

www.nhs.uk Set up over 60 years ago, it is now the largest provider of free health services in Europe.

NHS direct Helpline (England, Wales & NI). Tel: 0845 46 47 Telephone-based service of the NHS.

NHS Direct Helpline (Scotland). Tel: 0800 22 44 88

FOR INTERNATIONAL STUDENTS

www.ukcosa.org.uk Advice for international sudents.

www.educationuk.org British Council site listing courses in the UK and lots more.

www.fccollege.co.uk Central London college offering education services to UK and international students.

OTHER USEFUL CONTACT DETAILS

Postal services www.royalmail.com Tel: 08457 740 740 Find an address or postcode, track a parcel and get postal prices for all types of UK and international post.

British Association for Counselling and Psychotherapy 0870 443 5252

Relate (Relationship and sexual counselling/issues) 0845 130 4016

Alcoholics Anonymous 0845 769 7555

National Missing Persons Helpline 0500 700 700 www.missingpersons.org

BANKS

The main retail banks in the UK:

www.barclays.co.uk

www.lloydstsb.co.uk
www.hsbc.co.uk
www.natwest.co.uk

MAPS

www.streetmap.co.uk Enter a street name or postcode and this online service will bring up the relevant map.

BRITISH TOURIST AUTHORITY

www.visitbritain.com Provides details of all the interesting and beautiful places to visit in the UK.

EDUCATION

www.britishcouncil.org Information on UK education and can offer individual advice to those wanting to find a UK-based study course.

TRANSPORT

National Rail 0845 748 4950
Eurostar 01233 617 575
Eurotunnel 0870 535 3535
London Gatwick Airport 0870 0002468
London Heathrow Airport 0870 000 0123
London Luton Airport 01582 40 5100
London Stansted Airport 0870 000 0303
Virgin Trains 0845 722 2333
London Underground 020 7222 1234
Docklands Light Railway Hotline 020 7918 4000
British Telecom (BT) customer services 150 www.bt.com

Index